DISCOVERING AN ISLAND

The Roadside Heritage of the Isle of Wight

edited by
David Burdett & Allan Insole

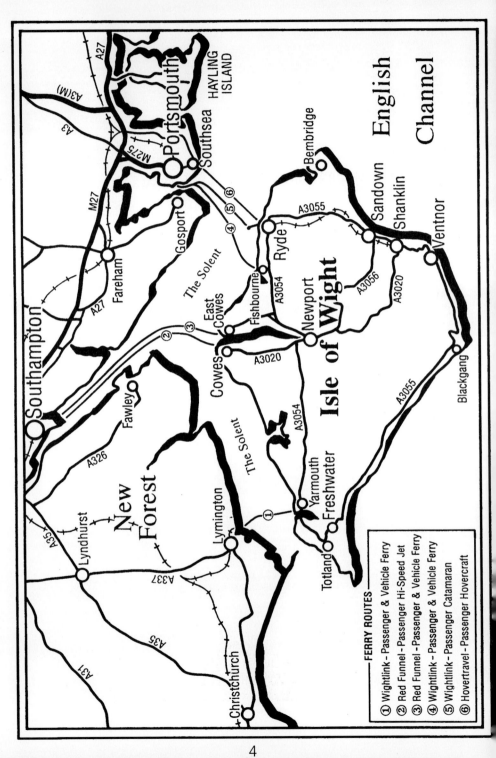

FERRY ROUTES
① Wightlink – Passenger & Vehicle Ferry
② Red Funnel – Passenger Hi-Speed Jet
③ Red Funnel – Passenger & Vehicle Ferry
④ Wightlink – Passenger & Vehicle Ferry
⑤ Wightlink – Passenger Catamaran
⑥ Hovertravel – Passenger Hovercraft

DISCOVERING AN ISLAND

The Roadside Heritage of the Isle of Wight

edited by
David Burdett & Allan Insole

ISLE of WIGHT SOCIETY

First published in Great Britain by The Isle of Wight Society
in association with Island Books

Series Editor Brian Hinton

Island Books is an imprint of Ravenswood Publications Ltd., London

ISBN 1 898198 12 8

British Library Cataloguing-in-Publishing Data
A catalogue record for this book is available from the British Library

Designed, printed and bound by Crossprint Design and Print
Newport, Isle of Wight, United Kingdom

Sole Distributor
HBS, Newport, Isle of Wight, United Kingdom

PREFACE

The favourable location of the Isle of Wight on the south coast of England, has made it a popular place to live for thousands of years. Man first arrived in the area over 100,000 years ago, long before the Island became separated from the English mainland. These early hunters and gatherers left no permanent mark to record their presence. About 8000 years ago, the area became an island in the English Channel as sea level rose after the end of the last Ice Age. Some 3000 years later, the first farmers arrived and began to clear patches in the primeval forest. These people left the oldest visible human monuments, the long barrows, as evidence of their occupation.

Subsequent prehistoric and historic inhabitants have all left their mark: the Romans left villas, medieval landowners founded great estates, manor houses and churches, while later farmers built stone houses and cottages. Wars down the centuries caused the construction of castles and forts. In the last century, the monarch of one of the largest empires the world has seen established her favourite home here. At the same time, the gentry and rich industrialists built their summer homes on the Island to take advantage of the mild climate.

The last century also saw the industrial era unleash the talents of thousands of local craftsmen who have built everything from rowing boats to space rockets here on the Island. At different times, local manufacturers have produced the fastest boat in the World, the largest aeroplane and, more recently, the fastest car.

Some aspect of this rich and diverse heritage is displayed in the various heritage exhibitions scattered around the Island. It is therefore possible to see items ranging from dinosaur footprints to a rocket testing site, all within the confines of this, the smallest English county. The main purpose of this book is therefore to help residents and visitors find their way to the fascinating collection of heritage exhibitions.

Many of the heritage displays which have been set up around the Island are run by local voluntary organisations. A lot of hard work has been put into these exhibitions by people who do it because of their love of the Island and its history. All exhibitions cost money in some way or another and all these organisations need to raise revenue for their ongoing expenses. One way of raising funds is by visitor's entrance fees or donations. A subsidiary purpose of the book is to encourage residents and visitors to take time to visit the exhibitions in the hope that their support will ensure the continued existence and improvement of the displays. Thereby we can enhance the appreciation of a fascinating Island.

Every effort has been made to trace the copyright owners of pictures used in this book. Information regarding errors or omissions will be welcomed by the publisher for inclusion or correction in future editions.

This book could not have been compiled without the encouragement and help of a great many organisations and individuals. Particular thanks are due to our wives, Sarah and Sarah, who have put up with long hours of debate and discussion; to John Barnes, Roy Brinton, Neil Hammerton, Jack & Joanna Jones, Jacqui Watts and Ron Winter for critically reading the early draft of the manuscript. To everyone else who has provided information and assistance we offer our grateful thanks. We also thank Peter Gustar, George Hook, Wayne Pritchett, Roger Smith, Sylvia Taylor and Eric Toogood for supplying photographs and Aubrey Carne for producing the maps.

CONTENTS

INDEX OF EXHIBITIONS BY LOCATION

INDEX OF EXHIBITIONS BY TOPIC

Discovering an Island
MAPS

INTRODUCTION

To plan a journey which will visit several of the heritage exhibitions is quite difficult since they are scattered all over the Island. However one is forced to admit that the road system radiates from Newport like spokes of a wheel with connecting roads joining the spokes. Combining this pattern with the Island's diamond shape, allows some form of organisation. Each of the four chapters which follow deals with a "facet of the diamond". Each is a circular tour which begins and ends at Newport and covers approximately a quarter of the Island. Route maps are provided at strategic points in the text to guide you from exhibition to exhibition.

In practice, it would not be possible to cover each "facet" within a single day and do justice to each exhibition. If you would rather devise your own itineraries, the various exhibitions and their locations are listed at the beginning of the book, together with the topics they cover.

Each exhibition has a standard entry within the text. Each entry provides the necessary basic information (location, opening times, etc.) which will enable you to plan your visit. While every effort has been made to ensure accuracy, various details (particularly admission charges) are liable to change. For that reason, the telephone numbers of the exhibitions have been included so that you can confirm that the information is still correct. The local Tourist Information Centres will also be able to provide up to date information. Also included in the standard entry for each exhibition is a description of the topic and an outline of the displays.

If you are following the trail, the text comments briefly on items of interest that you will pass along the way. These comments are just tasters to whet your appetite for more investigation into the heritage that helps to make the character of this delightful Island. If you wish to discover more details, a short booklist of useful publications can be found at the end of the book. A list of other sources of information is also provided.

The text assumes that the reader will be travelling by car. However, it is possible to follow the itineraries by using the local bus service. In addition, the Island possesses a comprehensive network of signposted footpaths. The Isle of Wight Council produces footpath maps and there are also several booklets describing local walks, all of which will help you explore the countryside on foot. Whether you are planning to see the Island by road or on foot you will find yourself passing near one of these exhibitions. So why not stop and find out more about the heritage of this beautiful county.

1 THE NORTH-EAST FACET

Newport — Whippingham — East Cowes — Ryde — Seaview — St. Helens — Bembridge — Brading—Binstead — Havenstreet — Downend (Robin Hill) — Newport

At the Lord Louis Library in Newport, located in Church Litten behind the bus station, you can purchase a copy of the "Newport Town Trail" which reveals the connections between the present buildings and activities of past centuries in the Island's capital town. The library building is modern but close to the east side is the memorial to the little sweep, Valentine Gray, whose sad story is recounted in the Town Trail. This memorial starts the walk.

1.1	Lord Louis Library

Reference Department has an area set aside for Isle of Wight reference material; first floor gallery is used to stage temporary exhibitions.

Location	Orchard Street, Newport (behind the bus station)
Operator	IW Council
Telephone no.	527655
Opening hours	9:00 am to 5:00 pm, Monday to Saturday
Admission charges	Free
Parking	Public car park by bus station
Bus route	Bus station 20 yards
Disabled access	Access for wheelchairs to ground floor only
Refreshments	Cafe in the bus station
Toilets	In the car park
Dogs	Guide dogs only

At the public car park next to the Lord Louis Library is a Tourist Information Centre. Here you can get information about the Newport Ghost Walks. These take place, weather permitting, on Wednesday

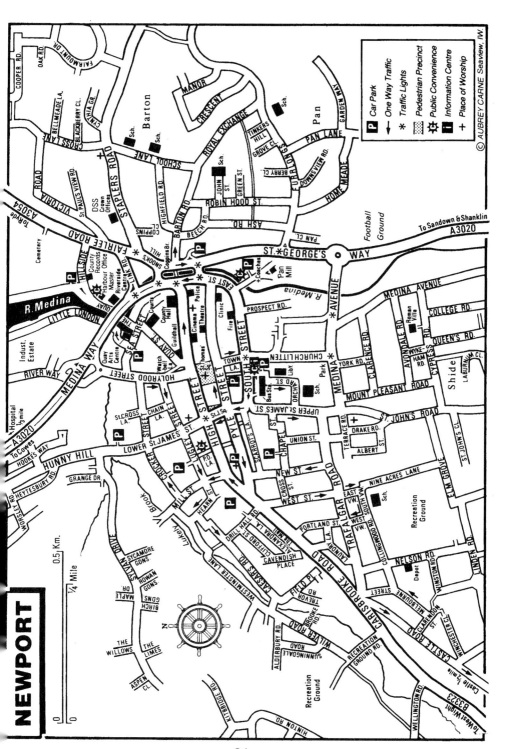

NEWPORT

© AUBREY CARNE Seaview, IW.

Legend:
- **P** Car Park
- One Way Traffic
- ✳ Traffic Lights
- Pedestrian Precinct
- ✿ Public Convenience
- **i** Information Centre
- ✝ Place of Worship

21

evenings and start at 8:00 pm from the Castle Inn located in the High Street.

At present there is no museum in the centre of Newport. However, the Isle of Wight Council intends to use the Guildhall at the junction of the High Street and Quay Street as a centre for its Cultural and Leisure Services Department. Part of the development will include a new museum devoted to the Island's archaeology and history.

A quarter of a mile from the bus station, away from the town centre and hidden among modern houses, you will find a Roman villa with an excellently preserved suite of baths.

1.2   Newport Roman Villa

3rd century Roman villa with a display of artefacts; reconstructed Roman garden; guided tours; souvenir and book shop.

Location	Cypress Road, Newport (off Medina Avenue)
Operator	IW Council
Telephone no.	529720
Opening hours	10:00 am to 5:30 pm (last admission 5:00 pm) daily, 1st April to 31st October; parties at other times by prior arrangement
Admission charges	Adults £1.50, children & senior citizens 75p
Parking	On street parking only; nearest public car park in Medina Avenue opposite Marks & Spencers
Bus route	Bus station 450 yards away
Disabled access	Suitable for wheelchairs
Refreshments	None
Toilets	None
Dogs	Not admitted

Another interesting place to visit in Newport is the Quay Arts Centre. This is housed in one of the last remaining 18th century quayside warehouses dating from the time when Newport was the main trading port of the Island. A small inner harbour basin, originally used by Mew's Brewery, was fed by the Lukely Brook. From the inner harbour a short canal runs through the buildings. The Arts Centre is mainly a venue for the visual arts but from time to time it mounts local heritage displays. A published diary of events is available.

Newport, at the head of the navigable portion of the Medina, has been a major port since medieval times. This photograph shows the 19th warehouses which originally stood on the eastern side of Town Quay, long since demolished. The railway viaduct on the left has been replaced by a dual carriageway. (Wayne Pritchett)

1.3   Quay Arts Centre

Exhibitions by local artists; sales of original works of art by local artists; occasional heritage exhibitions.

Location	Sea Street/Little London junction (near the harbour)
Operator	The Steve Ross Foundation for the Arts (a charity)
Telephone no.	528825
Opening hours	10:00 am to 5:00 pm, Monday to Saturday; 12:00 pm to 5:00 pm, Sundays
Admission charges	Free, except for some exhibitions when a small charge is made
Parking	Public car park opposite entrance
Bus route	Bus station 400 yards
Disabled access	Access for wheelchairs to ground floor only
Refreshments	Cafe in the Centre
Toilets	None
Dogs	Admitted on a lead

This very unusual bridge carried the railway line from Newport Station across the river Medina. One span, seen here partly open, could be wound back to allow sailing vessels to reach the warehouses which lay upstream. This bridge was replaced by the modern road bridge over the river. (Wayne Pritchett)

From the Quay Arts Centre, walk along Sea Street to Newport Harbour and turn left to pass under the road bridge. This bridge was built on the site of a viaduct which carried the Newport-Ryde and Newport-Sandown railway lines over the River Medina. On your right are the Harbour Master's offices at the top of a flight of steps. Here is a collection of maritime memorabilia. This can only be viewed when the Harbour Master or one of his staff are available. If the Master himself has time for a chat, which doesn't happen often, you will find that his memory of life on the river is full of interesting anecdotes. The building housing the Harbour Master's offices used to be the stables for the horses used by the Borough of Newport.

Below the Harbour Master's office there are public toilets. Next door to this building is the Riverside Centre. The building incorporates what was the pumping station for the Newport sewage works, which were built in 1895 following an outbreak of cholera. The present sewage treatment plant is about a mile to the north on the east bank of the Medina.

The sailing barge Gazelle *alongside the Newport Quay in about 1890. The Riverside Centre now stands where Sharpe's warehouse once stood and the gasworks has been demolished. (Allan Insole)*

Moving away from the Harbour Master's office and the road bridge, a narrow lane leads up to the main road. On your right is the County Records Office. Here the County Archivist can supply a great deal of information on the history of the Island and its inhabitants. There is also a large collection of books and pamphlets relating to all aspects of the Island which can be consulted for research purposes.

Looking across the main road, you can see the roof of a tall building. This houses the refurbished accommodation of the Department of Social Security offices. Part of the building used to be Nunn's lacemaking factory. In the 1840's about 800 women and children worked there and it was famous for the production of machine-made lace. It closed in the 1870's.

Turn left along the main A3054 road which leads to East Cowes. Continue out of Newport and at the end of the first straight section a signpost on the left advertises Island Harbour. Turn down the lane and proceed to the marina. The paddle steamer *Ryde Queen* is now berthed

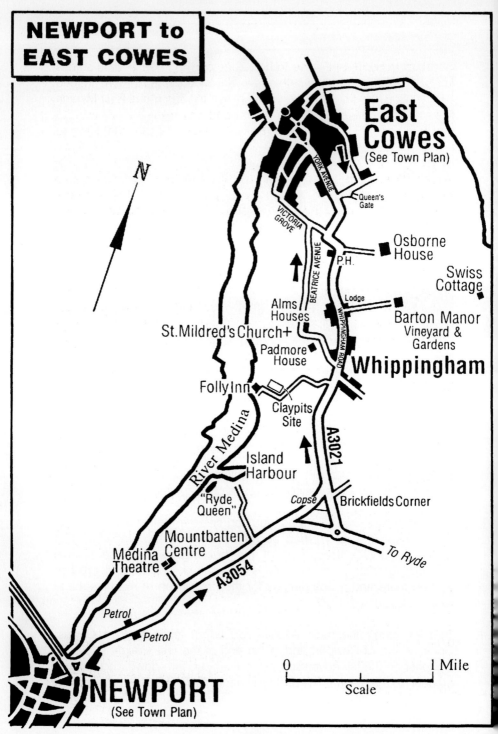

NEWPORT to EAST COWES

East Cowes
(See Town Plan)

YORK AVENUE

Queen's Gate

VICTORIA GROVE

BEATRICE AVENUE

P.H.

Osborne House

Swiss Cottage

Lodge

Alms Houses

WHIPPINGHAM ROAD

Barton Manor
Vineyard & Gardens

St.Mildred's Church+

Padmore House

Whippingham

Folly Inn

River Medina

Claypits Site

A3021

Island Harbour

"Ryde Queen"

Copse

Brickfields Corner

Mountbatten Centre

Medina Theatre

To Ryde

A3054

Petrol

Petrol

0   1 Mile

Scale

NEWPORT
(See Town Plan)

in a halftide pond. She used to be a ferry carrying passengers across the Solent between Portsmouth and Ryde. Near the mushroom shaped control house for the lock into the marina is the site of the East Medina tide mill. The marina occupies the mill pond into which the tide used to flow and ebb, driving the mill wheel. At the end of the road into the marina is the original elegant mill house.

Across the fields you can see a caravan site in the grounds of the house once owned by Uffa Fox, the well known yacht designer. He lived here after occupying one of the old Cowes chain ferries grounded on the beach at Kingston, near East Cowes.

Return to the main road, turn left and keep left at the next junction onto the A3021 towards East Cowes. At the following junction, Brickfields Corner, there is a copse on your right. Within this copse used to be the brickworks for the Osborne Estate. This was started in 1845 to supply bricks and, more importantly, land drainage pipes to the royal estate as Prince Albert gradually developed it.

Turn left towards East Cowes. Half way up the hill a signpost indicates The Folly Inn down a lane on the left. The lane is narrow and progress is restricted by road humps. However, there is a good vantage point with a fine view up the Medina River towards Newport. Further down the lane, the part of the caravan site on your right is known locally a the "Claypits site". It used to supply material to the local brickyards, probably including the Werrar works on the other side of the river. After passing the entrances to the caravan park, you arrive at the Folly Inn. Two hundred years ago a ship, *The Follie*, was stranded here. It was used as a house boat and the owner sold beer to those passing on foot or by boat. As the boat gradually collapsed, a building rose up around the remains. This expanded over the years until it reached its present status of Public House and Restaurant.

Returning up this lane to the first of the caravans, you will find a path leading off to the left through the woods and across the fields to Whippingham Church. This path is very old and has seen a lot of history, including a time in the Napoleonic Wars when the bodies of French prisoners were carried along it to the church for burial. Continue back to the main road, turn left then left again along a signposted lane to Saint Mildred's church.

There has been a church on this site since Saxon times. Nash added to the one standing at the beginning of the 19th century and also designed the building which later expanded to become the rectory. The church was rebuilt according to a design by Prince Albert when he was building up the Osborne and Barton estates. Across the road are the almshouses which were built by Queen Victoria in 1875 for pensioners of the royal household.

1.4	Saint Mildred's Church

Memorabilia of Queen Victoria and Prince Albert; exhibition in the church hall on local and royal history.

Location	Beatrice Avenue (between East Cowes and Whippingham)
Operator	Whippingham Parish Church Council
Telephone no.	298175
Opening hours	10:00 am to 4:00 pm, Monday to Friday, 1st April to 31st October
Admission charges	Free
Parking	Car park by church hall
Bus route	Southern Vectis nos. 4 & 5; bus stop by school, walk north along main road and then take path CS25 left across field.
Disabled access	Access for wheelchairs
Refreshments	Tuck shop near church
Toilets	In church yard
Dogs	Not allowed

Beatrice Avenue, leading from the church towards East Cowes, provides a pleasant view of the Medina valley on the left. Many street names in East Cowes recall the days when Queen Victoria and her family lived here. For a considerable part of each year, Queen Victoria ruled one of the largest empires the world has ever seen from Osborne House. At the end of Beatrice Avenue turn left into Victoria Grove. Continue down the hill and follow the right-hand bend at the bottom into Adelaide Grove. At the end of this, turn left again down York Avenue and park opposite the large building labelled Town Hall, which is now the East Cowes Community Centre.

Slip at Marvin's Minerva Yard, East Cowes in the foreground with their Shambler's Yard in West Cowes on the opposite bank of the Medina, 1908. Boat- and shipbuilding in East and West Cowes go back to at least Elizabethan times, with both naval and civilian vessels being built. Marvin's had premises on both sides of the river and at the end of the 19th century were one of the largest yacht repair yards in Britain. (Allan Insole)

East Cowes has developed rapidly in the last two hundred years and passed through several distinct phases. An exhibition of various aspects of this history can be seen at the East Cowes Heritage Centre in Clarence Road. Copies of "Discovering East Cowes" can be purchased at the Centre. This booklet describes three separate walks around the town.

1.5   East Cowes Heritage Centre

Exhibition showing development of East Cowes; changing exhibitions of local history; books of old photographs of the town; videos of old films of the area; children's corner.

Location	8, Clarence Road, East Cowes
Operator	East Cowes Heritage Organisation

Telephone no.	280310 between 10:00 am and 1:00 pm; 293010 (J. Barnes) or 296718 (D. Burdett)
Opening hours	10:00 am to 1:00 pm, Tuesday to Saturday, 1st February to 23rd December
Admission charges	Free
Parking	On street, 50 yds, opposite Community Centre in York Avenue
Bus route	Southern Vectis nos. 4 & 5
Disabled access	Wheelchair access
Refreshments	Cafes in York Avenue and Castle Street
Toilets	Next to Community Centre
Dogs	On a lead

On East Cowes seafront is one of the two propellers which drove *HMS Cavalier*. This destroyer was one of several built at East Cowes by J.S. White's shipyard during the Second World War and held the record of the fastest ship in the Royal Navy for 25 years. *HMS Cavalier* is the last remaining Second World War destroyer and is being preserved at Hebburn by South Tyneside Council.

From the seafront, go up Cambridge Road to Old Road. This was the original road from East Cowes to Newport. Go a short distance up Old Road and then turn right into Hefford Road. This leads up through a modern development of bungalows until, on the right, is an flat open grassy area. This is the site of East Cowes Castle, developed by Nash for his own use between 1798 and 1835. Here Nash entertained lavishly, the Prince Regent and the painter Turner being amongst the many guests.

Cross-section and plan of a typical icehouse. Ice was stored in the well a buried in the earth; b, c and d are pit, conduit and well to take any water that may be formed. The store was entered through a long tunnel in which there were a series of doors. (From The Englishman's Garden, *1875)*

At the end of Hefford Road, turn left into Sylvan Avenue. A few yards up the hill on the left is a grass-covered mound between the road and house number 85. This mound covers the remains of an ice house that served East Cowes Castle. Ice houses were used to store ice collected in the winter through into the following summer. The ice was used to cool drinks, make ice cream and preserve food.

At the top of Sylvan Avenue, turn right into Old Road. At the bend is the Queens Gate, the royal entrance to Osborne House. To visit the house, turn left into the wide thoroughfare of York Avenue and carry on to the tradesman's entrance on the double bend opposite the Prince of Wales public house.

1.6	Osborne House

Queen Victoria's favourite home and grounds, including the royal children's summer house "Swiss Cottage" which can be reached by horsedrawn carriage; bookable education room in the House.

Location	York Avenue, East Cowes
Operator	English Heritage
Telephone no.	200022
Opening hours	10:00 am to 6:00 pm, daily, 1st April to 31st October
Admission charges	Adults £5.50, children £2.75, senior citizens £4.10; free to English Heritage members Grounds only: adults £2.60, children £1.30, senior citizens £1.95. Special party rates available. (Also available, combined entrance ticket for both Osborne House and Barton Manor: adults £8.60, children £2.61, senior citizens £6.85)
Parking	Car park in grounds
Bus route	Southern Vectis nos. 4 & 5
Disabled access	Wheelchairs access to grounds and ground floor of house only
Refreshments	Cafe by car park
Toilets	In the car park, at reception area at Swiss Cottage
Dogs	On a lead in the grounds only

From the entrance to the grounds of Osborne, turn left. Continue along Whippingham Road for about half a mile until two lodge houses are seen on the left. Turn left into the driveway between the lodges. This leads you to Barton Manor and its farmhouse, the core of a model farm estate developed by Prince Albert in the 1850's. It is now the home of Robert Stigwood, the famous impresario.

Video presentation explaining part of Barton's history under royal ownership. Barton Manor is now an award-winning vineyard, taste famous award winning wine for free from free souvenir glass. Beautiful gardens, rose hedge maze and well stocked lake with tame fish and a collection of waterfowl. Display of paintings of exotic flora. Listen to the music while browsing amongst a large collection of memorabilia of stage, screen and music (including platinum, gold and silver discs).

Location	Whippingham Road (between East Cowes and Whippingham)
Operator	Barton Manor Gardens and Vineyard Ltd
Telephone no.	292835
Opening hours	10:30 am to 5:30 pm, daily, 1st April to 2nd Sunday in October
Admission charges	Adults £3.75, children under 15 years old when accompanied by an adult, senior citizens 3.20. (Also available, combined entrance ticket for both Osborne House and Barton Manor: adults £8.60, children £2.61, senior citizens £6.85)
Parking	Car park at end of drive
Bus route	Southern Vectis nos. 4 & 5
Disabled access	Wheelchairs access to grounds and ground floor of house only
Refreshments	Cafe in grounds
Toilets	Next to cafe
Dogs	Guide dogs only

Leave the drive of Barton Manor and turn left towards Whippingham. The group of modern houses on the left occupies an area that once resounded to deafening roars while blinding flashes lit up the sky and the surrounding countryside as a battery of 4.3 inch anti-aircraft guns attempted to drive off the Luftwaffe as it attacked the shipyards of Cowes and East Cowes during the Second World War. At night, some aircraft used the Medina as a navigation aid after attacking or after being driven away from Southampton or Portsmouth. The underground bunkers and ammunition stores associated with the anti-aircraft battery were so solidly built that, when hostilities ended, they could not be destroyed and the land could not be returned to agricultural use. This is the highest point on the East Cowes peninsular, with views across the Solent to Portsmouth.

Continuing past the houses, the ornate roof of the Bavarian-styled Coburg Cottage can be seen across the fields on the left. This was once in the middle of the Barton Estate. It was completed in 1874 as estate worker's cottages. Although Prince Albert came from Coburg, the design is surprising since it was actually completed thirteen years after his death.

At Whippingham Forge, turn left into Alverstone Road. This road passes through a mix of bungalows and houses which are part of the village of Whippingham. The name appears to originate from the early 8th century when it was known as Wippa's Ham. It makes one wonder about earlier settlements here which were sufficiently important to have had a church since Saxon times.

Continuing along Alverstone Road, you come to a cross-roads at an entrance to the Barton Estate. Alverstone Road bears right but the itinerary carries straight on along Brock's Copse Road. This plunges down the hill through an arboreal tunnel towards the stream called Palmer's Brook. Half way down the hill is one of two lodges, built in 1867, along the Osborne Estate Boundary Drive. This drive started at Barton Manor. It went down the hill to the foreshore, then turned south along Palmer's Brook, through Brock's Copse and on to the Ryde Road opposite Palmer's Farm, where the second lodge was built. This drive was subsequently used by Queen Victoria to travel to Whippingham Station on the one occasion she travelled to Ventnor by train to visit the Royal National Hospital for Diseases of the Chest.

At the top of the hill on the eastern side of the stream is Wootton. At the end of Brock's Copse Road, turn left along Palmers Road and then take the second turning on the right, Church Road. At the bottom of the road is the Norman church of Saint Edmund. In 1800, this was the centre of what was then the rather remote village of Wootton. In 1969, about 200,000 people flocked to a field 200 yards from the church for the Isle of Wight Festival of Music, the second of three pop festivals held on the Island. The first was held at a farm between Godshill and Niton in 1968 and attracted 10,000 people. The third and most famous gathering was

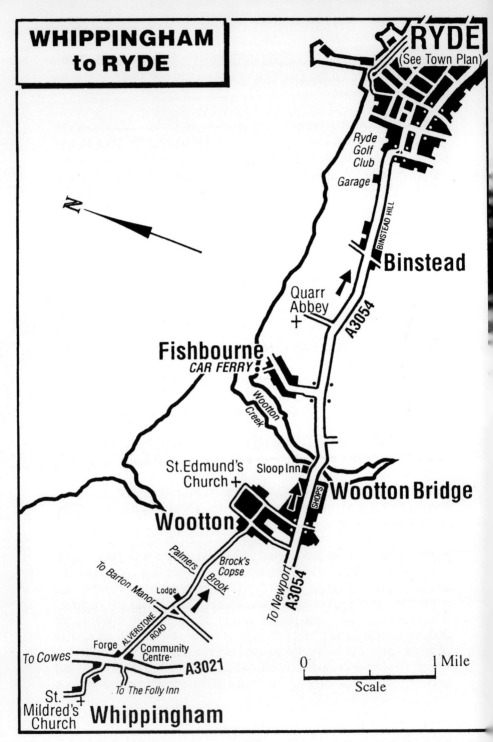

WHIPPINGHAM to RYDE

RYDE
(See Town Plan)

Ryde Golf Club

Garage

BINSTEAD HILL

Binstead

Quarr Abbey +

A3054

Fishbourne
CAR FERRY

Wootton Creek

St. Edmund's Church +

Sloop Inn

SHOPS

Wootton Bridge

Wootton

Palmers

Brock's Copse

Brook

To Barton Manor

Lodge

To Newport

A3054

ALVERSTONE ROAD

Forge

To Cowes

Community Centre

A3021

To The Folly Inn

St. Mildred's Church +

Whippingham

0 _____ 1 Mile
Scale

held at Afton Down, near Freshwater, in 1970 and brought over 300,000 fans to the Island - three times the normal population.

Turn right at the church to reach the main A3054 road. Turn left down the hill to Wootton Creek. On the left is the Sloop Inn. The new houses just beyond it were built on the site of a tide mill powered by two undershot wheels. These wheels were fed by water which passed under the causeway into Wootton Creek. Hence the area became known as Wootton Bridge.

Wootton Bridge Tide Mill about 1900, one of a number of large tide mills built in the late 18th century to provide the increased quantity of flour required by the Island's increasing population. As the tide rose, water flowed up Wootton Creek and under Wootton Bridge which acted as a mill dam. As the tide fell, the sluices beneath the causeway were closed and water flowed back to Wootton Creek past two millwheels which drove the machinery. This mill was demolished in 1962. (Sylvia Taylor)

From Wootton Creek, continue towards Ryde along the A3054. After about three quarters of a mile is a junction with traffic lights. The road to the left, Fishbourne Lane, leads down to the Wightlink car ferry terminal. The entrance to Wootton Creek has been important since prehistoric times. The area has been the subject of a recent archaeological survey as part of a study of the Solent coastline of the Island. Anyone interested in the findings should contact the IW Archaeological Centre (61 Clatterford Road, Carisbrooke; tel. 529963).

A further quarter of a mile towards Ryde is the entrance to the tree-lined drive to Quarr Abbey. The present church of the Benedictine Abbey of Quarr was consecrated in 1912. The community took refuge on the Island after coming over from France and settled initially at Appuldurcombe. However, the Quarr site has a much older ecclesiastical association since in 1132 a Cistercian Abbey was founded here. Stone from the local quarries was used in the construction of Winchester and Chichester Cathedrals, Romsey Abbey and many small parish churches in Hampshire and West Sussex. In 1536, the abbey was dissolved and much of the stonework sold off - some being used to build East and West Cowes Castles - the Cowes. Some of the original monastic settlement remains, as well as a fishpond, one of a series built along a stream to the south of the main road.

Quarr Abbey buildings about 1900 after the remnant of the original medieval building had been converted into a farmhouse. (Allan Insole)

In medieval times, Ryde belonged to the Manor of Ashey which was owned by the Abbey of Wherwell, near Andover. The original boundaries were Monkton-mead Brook and Smallbrook to the east, the Downs to the south and Binstead Stream to the west. The northern boundary was defined by 'a line as far into the sea beyond low water as a man could reach the ground with an oar of 18 feet'. Over the centuries, two separate hamlets, Upper and Lower Ryde, gradually developed. These became one in 1780 when William Player laid out Union Street. Ryde then began to attract "genteel" company, being a near neighbour of Portsmouth. The town expanded rapidly, building leases being granted on the Player's Estate from 1810 onwards. In 1814, the first pier was opened to facilitate landing. Prior to this, getting ashore involved a long walk across wet sand at low tide - women were often carried ashore by uncouth seamen. Between 1827 and 1832 the Town Hall, Saint Thomas's Chapel and Brigstocke Terrace, all designed by John Sanderson, were built, together with many villas of a similarly elegant design. The Esplanade came later in 1856 and the canoe lake in 1880.

Ryde piers and Esplanade Station, 1908. The Ryde Pier on the right is actually a composite structure comprising a pedestrian/vehicle pier, a railway pier and, between them, a tramway pier. The origins of the pedestrian/vehicle pier date back to 1814, making it the first major piled passenger pier and the ancestor of all seaside piers. On the far right is the head of the Victorian Pier built in 1859 and demolished in 1922. Between the two piers is the town quay, with a small crane standing on it, and the horse boat slip, now the landing slip for cross-Solent hovercraft. (Allan Insole)

The Eastern Esplanade Pavilion, now part of the L.A. Bowl, was built during the depression years of 1926 and 1927. In 1656 the population of Ryde was 220 persons, in 1801 it was 900 persons and by 1971 it had reached 23,171. A Ryde Town Trail is available. It may be obtained from the Tourist Information Centre located at the bottom of George Street where it meets the Esplanade.

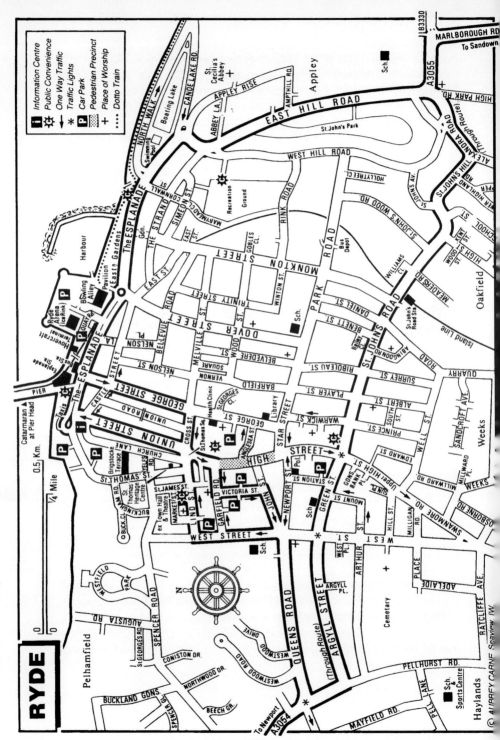

RYDE

Pelhamfield

Appley

Oakfield

Weeks

Haylands

© AUBREY CARNE Seaview I.W.

In 1987 the Queen visited the Island to mark the bicentenary of the sailing of the first convict ship to Australia from Spithead. This event is commemorated in the gardens of Saint Thomas' Chapel. The church is no longer consecrated and the building is used to house an exhibition.

1.8	Saint Thomas' Heritage Centre

Exhibition about the transportation of convicts to Australia in the 19th century, sited in the disused private chapel of the Brigstocke Estate.

Location	Saint Thomas' Street (off St. Thomas' Square at the top of Union Street)
Operator	Saint Thomas' Trust and Friends of St. Thomas' (a charity)
Telephone no.	882459 / 872395
Opening hours	10:00 am to 4:00 pm, Easter to 30th September
Admission charges	Free
Parking	Public car parks by Town Hall in Lind Street and at bottom of St. Thomas' Street
Bus route	Southern Vectis nos.1, 1A, 4, 7, 7A, 7B, 7C, 8, 10 & 88
Disabled access	Access for wheelchairs
Refreshments	Cafes and restaurants in Union Street
Toilets	In the building
Dogs	Admitted

The itinerary leaves Ryde along the Esplanade towards Puckpool. At the end of the Esplanade, by the paddling pool, the road turns inland and up the hill. At the top of the hill, take the B3330 off to the left towards Seaview and Nettlestone. After a quarter of a mile there is a signposted turning on the left to Puckpool.

The road winds down the hill to the entrance to Puckpool Battery on the left. The battery is unusual because it was designed specifically to fire mortar shells in order to protect the valuable anchorage off Portsmouth. In addition to containing recreational facilities the battery houses the Puckpool Park Wireless Museum.

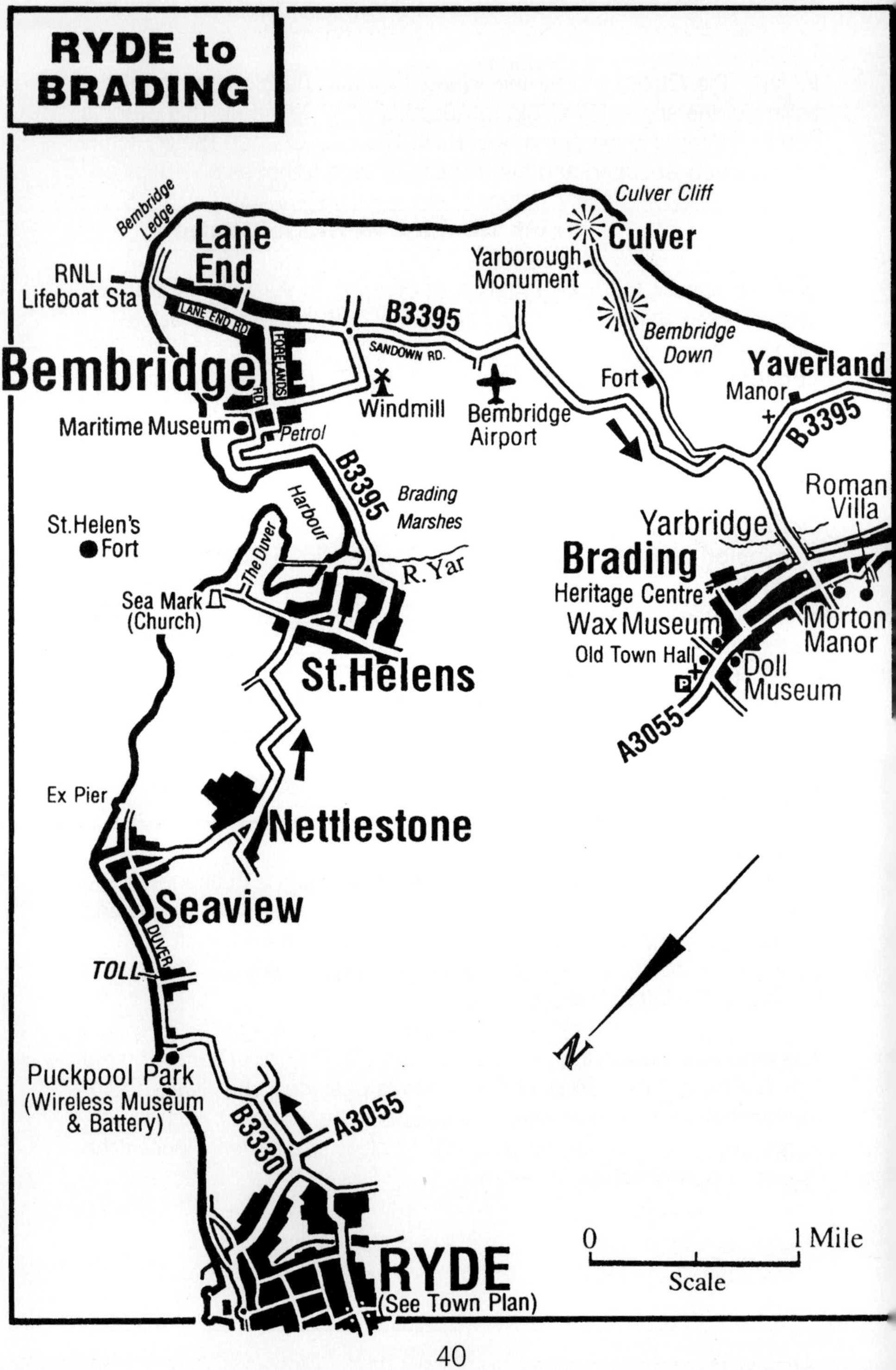

RYDE to BRADING

Bembridge Ledge

RNLI
Lifeboat Sta

Lane End

Culver Cliff

Yarborough
Monument

Culver

B3395

LANE END RD.

SANDOWN RD.

LHIGHLANDS RD.

Bembridge

Bembridge Down

Yaverland

Fort

Manor
+

B3395

Maritime Museum

Petrol

Windmill

Bembridge
Airport

Roman
Villa

Harbour

B3395

Brading Marshes

Yarbridge

Brading

St.Helen's
Fort

The Duver

R. Yar

Heritage Centre

Wax Museum

Morton
Manor

Sea Mark
(Church)

Old Town Hall

Doll
Museum

St.Helens

P

A3055

Ex Pier

Nettlestone

Seaview

DUVER

TOLL

N

Puckpool Park
(Wireless Museum
& Battery)

B3330

A3055

RYDE
(See Town Plan)

0	1 Mile

Scale

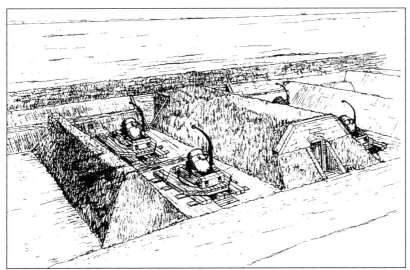

View of 13in. Mortar bay at Puckpool Battery, 1872. (Drawing by Peter Sprack and used with the permission of The Redoubt Consultancy)

1.9   Puckpool Battery

Mortar battery; views from the gun emplacements; recreation ground.

Location	Puckpool Hill, Seaview
Operator	IW Council
Telephone no.	520000
Opening hours	8:00 am to 6:00 pm in winter, all hours in summer
Admission charges	Free
Parking	Outside the gates and in the grounds
Bus route	Southern Vectis no.8
Disabled access	Wheelchair access to the grounds but not on the fortifications
Refreshments	Cafe in the grounds open 9:00 am to 9:00 pm in summer
Toilets	In the grounds
Dogs	Admitted

The history of radio and television demonstrated by the real thing. Annual events: International Marconi Day commemoration at Puckpool Park in April; Wight Wireless Rally at Arreton Manor in September.

Location	On the left, just inside the gates to Puckpool Park
Operator	Communications and Electronics Museum Trust (a charity)
Telephone no.	567665
Opening hours	2:00 pm to 4:00 pm, daily, Easter to end September; 2:00 pm to 4:00 pm, Sundays only in winter
Admission charges	Free
Parking	Outside the gates and in the grounds
Bus route	Southern Vectis no.8
Disabled access	Wheelchair access
Refreshments	Cafe in the park
Toilets	In the park
Dogs	Admitted

From Puckpool, the route continues along the road behind the beach towards Seaview. This toll road runs along the top of an embankment (The Duver) built in 1800 across a natural harbour mouth. For the following twenty years the area behind The Duver was used for salt production. Sea water was allowed into large ponds in the summer. The brine produced by evaporation was further concentrated by boiling to form salt crystals. At the end of The Duver the road turns right. Immediately on the right are Salterns Cottages, a row of workers cottages which had a brine boiling house at the southern end.

A short walk eastward along the beach from Seaview is the site of the elegant Seaview Chain Pier. This was one of only two piers built on the principle of a suspension bridge. Unfortunately, it was destroyed in a storm in 1952 and only the anchorage points for the landward chains can be seen today.

From Seaview, proceed up the hill through Nettlestone to St Helen's. On entering the village, take a sharp left bend down the hill towards the

The 1000 foot long Seaview Chain Pier was built between 1879 and 1881, the pier head being added in 1889. It was one of only two piers built on the suspension bridge principle, the other being at Brighton. This elegant structure was wrecked by a severe gale in December, 1951 and the remains were removed the following year. (George Hook)

sandy spit of land known as The Duver. There is a car park on the spit. The land was made a golf course in Edwardian times but the property now belongs to the National Trust, the old club house being a National Trust holiday cottage! On the sea front, there are a number of old railway carriages which used to carry tourists on the local railway lines. Today they are being used as beach chalets. In the summer, you may be able to spot some almost original interiors through the open doors.

The old church at the end of the beach fell into disrepair after the dissolution of the monasteries in 1536, but the tower continued to be used as a sea mark, aiding navigation into Brading Haven. Stones from the church were used to whiten the decks of the Men-o'-War lying in the anchorage - hence the term "holystoning the decks". Take the footpath inland towards the harbour. After crossing an area of flat grassland, a large lagoon is reached. This was the millpond for the St. Helen's Tidemill.

Return to the green around which St. Helen's is built and take the left turn, the B3395, towards Bembridge (Station Road). This runs downhill towards Bembridge Harbour. On the right, at the bottom of the hill, is the old St. Helen's Railway station, now a private house. On the left is the site of the old railway quay where Southern Railway vessels used to discharge coal for use on the Island's railway system.

St. Helen's Quay was developed in the late 19th century as a replacement for Brading Quay. It was a major port for the import of coal for both the Island railways and for the local gasworks, which stood close to the quay. Between 1885 and 1888, it was also the Island terminus of a train ferry service from Langstone Harbour. (Sylvia Taylor)

Brading Haven was an important natural harbour from Roman times onwards and the quay at Brading was used by large vessels. This painting by William Daniell gives an impression of the haven as it was in 1823, before the construction of the embankment between Bembridge and St. Helens and the subsequent draining of Brading Marshes between 1874 and 1879. (Allan Insole)

The main road now runs out onto an embankment between Bembridge Harbour and Brading Marshes. Until surprisingly recently, the area to the south of this embankment was a large natural harbour and the town of Brading was a busy port. Over the years, the harbour gradually silted up until it became unusable by large vessels. After several attempts, an embankment was finally constructed between St. Helen's and

Bembridge in 1878 and the original harbour was reclaimed. At the St. Helen's end of the embankment, the road crosses a bridge beside which are sluice gates that drain the water from this land and stop the sea from reflooding what was once the largest harbour on the Island.

Continue along the top of the embankment. At the end of it, the road turns right and climbs a low hill into the village of Bembridge. On the left, at the top of the rise is a museum housing a significant collection devoted to the maritime activities of the past.

1.11 Shipwreck Centre and Maritime Museum

Six galleries of displays including pirate gold and silver, Spanish pieces of eight; antique diving equipment; ship models; videos of lifeboat rescues and diving operations; RNLI history; artefacts from local shipwrecks, including an account of discovery of *HMS Swordfish*, a submarine lost off Bembridge in 1940. Shop with wide range of books, gifts and souvenirs

Location	Sherbourne Street, Bembridge
Operator	Mr & Mrs M Woodward
Telephone no.	872223/873125
Opening hours	10:00 am to 5:00 pm, daily, late March to late October
Admission charges	Adults £2.10, children £1.35, senior citizens £1.50; family and party rates
Parking	On street
Bus route	Southern Vectis nos. 7, 7A & 90
Disabled access	Wheelchair access to ground floor only
Refreshments	Squarerigger Restaurant opposite
Toilets	100 yards
Dogs	Not admitted

From the museum, turn left towards the junction with High Street. Turn right here, then left into Forelands Road. Continue until you reach Lane End Road on the left. At the end of this road is Bembridge Lifeboat Station. This area is hazardous for shipping because of the rocks of Bembridge Ledge and the complex local tidal streams. A record of the services that have been provided by the Bembridge Lifeboat are on display at the station.

1.12	Bembridge Lifeboat Station

Example of both inshore and offshore lifeboats on station; extensive collection of photographs in inshore lifeboat house showing the history of the Bembridge Lifeboat station; souvenir and book shop next to lifeboat buildings. Good views towards the Nab Tower and Portsmouth.

Location	Seaward end of Lane End Road
Operator	The Royal National Lifeboat Institute (a charity)
Telephone no.	873292 (Honorary Secretary)
Opening hours	2:00 pm to 4:00 pm, Wed, Thurs and Sun and at other times if station manned, 1st May to 30th September. Actual opening hours are subject to operational commitments, the station being on call 24 hours a day throughout the year
Admission charges	Free (donations accepted)
Parking	By the lifeboat station
Bus route	Southern Vectis no.7, 7A & 90
Disabled access	Wheelchair access to inshore rigid inflatable boathouse only
Refreshments	Cafe across car park
Toilets	10 yards
Dogs	Admitted

From the lifeboat station, on a clear day, you can see the Nab Tower four and three quarter miles away. This is a concrete and steel structure standing in fifteen metres of water. It shows a navigation light at a height of 27 metres above the sea. The tower is the last of three such structures that were being built at Shoreham during the First World War. A series of these towers were designed to form anti-submarine defences across the English Channel. However, they were never installed. At the end of hostilities, it was decided to use the one completed tower as a navigation mark at the entrance to Spithead which was then even busier than it is today.

Return along Lane End Road and continue straight on along Steyne Road. After nearly half a mile, at a roundabout, there is a sign to the right indicating Bembridge Windmill. It is the only surviving windmill on the Island and dates from the 1700's.

1.13	**Bembridge Windmill**

Last surviving windmill on the Island; much of the original milling machinery remains inside the building; energetic and interesting climb to the top.

Location	Kings Road, Bembridge
Operator	The National Trust (a charity)
Telephone no.	873945
Opening hours	10:00 am to 5:00 pm, daily, July & August; 10:00 am to 5:00 pm, Sunday to Friday, 30th March - 30th October
Admission charges	Adults £1.20, children 60p; free to National Trust members
Parking	100 yards
Bus route	Southern Vectis no. 7, 7A & 90
Disabled access	Wheelchair access to exterior only
Refreshments	None
Toilets	None
Dogs	Not admitted

Return to the roundabout and turn right onto Sandown Road. This road winds downhill and then passes Bembridge Airport. This was constructed in 1922 and was used for passenger services to London in the 1930's. The present hangars were built in the 1960's.

Half a mile beyond the airfield, on a sharp left hand bend, there is a narrow lane leading back on the left. This lane climbs steeply to the top of Bembridge Down, where there it passes a number of features. Firstly, there is Bembridge Fort which dates back to the 1850's. Then the conspicuous monument to the Earl of Yarborough, the first Commodore of the Royal Yacht Squadron. Finally, beyond a public house and the old coastguard cottages, are there are the remains of Culver Battery, a Second World War structure. There are several car parks along the crest of the Down and the views from the top of the down on a clear day are magnificent.

Retrace the route back to the main road and turn left. Further on, on the left, is Yaverland Manor. Yaverland has two entries in the Domesday Book, both referring back to the time of its ownership during the reign of Edward the Confessor when each part was valued at 100 shillings. The manor dates back to pre-Norman times. In the 16th century, the earlier Norman house was rebuilt using much of the original structure. One wall is over six feet thick. The date inscribed on the staircase arch is 1620 when the rebuilding is believed to have been completed. Through the trees, it is possible to see the Norman parish church which used to be the private chapel of the manor house.

Bembridge and Yaverland were originally cut off at each high tide from the rest of the Island. It was not until the 13th century that a causeway and bridge across the tidal marshes were built at Yarbridge by Sir William Russell. The modern road runs along the top of the causeway and over the narrow bridge just before crossing the railway line. At the traffic lights continue straight ahead. At the bend in the road a lane to the left leads to Morton Manor. The Manor House, dating back to 1249, was largely rebuilt in 1680.

Sheep washing at Yarbridge, about 1900. The purpose of this process was to remove grease from the fleece before the animals were sheared and was always done in running water. (Allan Insole)

1.14 Morton Manor

Family home dating back to 1249 classically furnished in period style; rose and Elizabethan sunken gardens; vineyard, winery and wine museum; children's play area; shop.

Location	Morton Old Road, Yarbridge, Brading
Operator	Mr & Mrs J.B. Trzebski
Telephone no.	406168
Opening hours	10:00 am to 5:30 pm, Sunday to Friday, Good Friday to last Saturday in October
Admission charges	Adults £3.00, children £1.00, senior citizens £2.60,
Parking	In grounds
Bus route	Southern Vectis nos. 16 &16B to Yarbridge
Disabled access	Wheelchair access
Refreshments	Tea rooms
Toilets	In the grounds
Dogs	On lead in the grounds; guide dogs only in the house

Exiting Morton Manor grounds, turn right and then right again to Brading Roman Villa. Only part of this very large villa has been excavated. It is believed to have been the centre of a rich and prosperous farming estate and the remnants of the original fields can be seen on the slopes of Brading Down above. It had fine mosaic floors, painted walls and luxury objects of pottery and glass were imported during the period of occupation. The site has suffered in the recent past due to flooding but is still considered to be the twelfth most important Roman site in the Britain. Currently English Heritage are carrying out extensive work with the trustees to improve the site.

1.15 Brading Roman Villa

Excavated west wing of a large Roman villa is displayed under cover with some fine examples of mosaic floors; worksheets for school parties and guided tours by arrangement.

Location	Off Morton Old Road, near Yarbridge, Brading
Operator	The Oglander Trust
Telephone no.	406223
Opening hours	10:00 am to 5:30 pm, Monday to Saturday and 10:30 am to 5:30 pm Sundays, April to September
Admission charges	Adults £1.50, children 85p
Parking	On site
Bus route	Southern Vectis nos. 16 & 16B to Yarbridge
Disabled access	Wheelchair access
Refreshments	None on site; picnic area
Toilets	On site
Dogs	Not admitted

Return to the traffic lights on the main road. Turn left along New Road to the petrol station on the right. Turn right into Station Road and continue to the station buildings where the Brading Heritage Centre is located.

1.16 Brading Heritage Centre

Exhibition of local history and railway history; local footpath trails on sale.

Location	Brading Railway Station
Operator	Brading Station Community Centre Association
Telephone no.	407693
Opening hours	1st May to 31st September
Admission charges	Free
Parking	Station forecourt
Bus route	Southern Vectis nos. 16 & 16B 88
Disabled access	Wheelchair access
Refreshments	None
Toilets	In station
Dogs	Admitted

Return to the main road and carry straight on, passing the pedestrian crossing. On the left side of the road is a bull-ring. The ring used to be sited in the middle of the road but was recently moved to its present location. It was used to secure a bull while it was baited by dogs. At one time the baiting of a bull before it was slaughtered was a legal requirement to ensure the quality of the meat. Anybody who slaughtered a bull without baiting it was fined.

Continue through the town to the church of St. Mary The Virgin, just past which is a large public car park. The church was founded in Saxon times. Inside you can obtain more information about the history of the church. From the church, walk a few yards to Brading Town Hall where the original stocks can be seen. In the room above is a museum.

1.17   Brading Old Town Hall & Stocks

Photographs, documents and artefacts outline the history of this historic town.

Location	High Street, Brading
Operator	Brading Town Trust
Telephone no.	407669
Opening hours	11:00 am to 4:00 pm, Sunday to Friday, Whitsun to mid-September
Admission charges	Adults 50p, children 30p
Parking	Public car park by the church
Bus route	Southern Vectis nos. 16 & 16B
Disabled access	Wheelchair access to stocks only
Refreshments	Cafes nearby
Toilets	In car park
Dogs	Admitted on a lead

Across Wall Lane from the old Town Hall is the Wax Museum. This is housed in a very old timber frame building, the only surviving example of close studding construction on the Island.

1.18   Wax Museum

House includes 'Ancient Rectory Mansion' c.1066 A.D., with its galleried courtyards, lover's balcony, Kissing Arch, Priest Hole and wishing fountains. The Wax Museum, depicts famous and infamous characters in Island history. There is also a Chamber of Horrors, set in the Castle Dungeons and a second museum - Animal World of Natural History - alongside, included free.

Location	High Street, Brading
Operator	Investment Securities Ltd.
Telephone no.	407286
Opening hours	10:00 a.m. to 10:00 p.m., daily in the summer; 10:00 a.m. to 5:00 p.m. daily between Oct. and April
Admission charges	Adults £4.25, children £2.75
Parking	Free car park at rear of building, plus large public car park by church
Bus route	Southern Vectis nos. 16 & 16B
Disabled access	Wheelchair access to groundfloor only
Refreshments	Cafes nearby
Toilets	Tiolets and baby changing facilities on site
Dogs	Dogs allowed

Walk down the narrow Wall Lane between the old Town Hall and the Wax Museum. On the left, in the corner of the churchyard is a cattle pound, where stray cattle were penned until claimed. At the end of Wall Lane there was once a quay, now hidden, dating to the times when Brading was the most important port of the Island. The wall which crosses the marshes from the end of Wall Lane to Centurion's Copse is an old sea wall dating back to the 17th century. The wall and the two sets of sluice gates in it were used to drain the land to the south. The name "Centurion" is probably a corruption of St. Urian since there used to be a chapel dedicated him in the area.

On the opposite side of the High Street to the Wax Museum is the Lilliput Museum of Antique Dolls and Toys.

1.19	Lilliput Antique Doll and Toy Museum

One of Britain's finest collections of antique dolls and toys with exhibits dating from 2000 B.C. to 1945; educational talks; gift shop; worksheets and guide book available.

Location	High Street, Brading
Operator	Graham Munday
Telephone no.	407231
Opening hours	10:00 am to 5:00 pm, daily, early March to mid-January; 9:30am to 9:30pm in summer season

Admission charges	Adults £1.35, children and senior citizens 95p, under 5 years old free
Parking	Public car park 200 yards next to church
Bus route	Southern Vectis nos. 16 & 16B
Disabled access	Ramps provided on request for wheelchairs
Refreshments	Cafes nearby
Toilets	In car park
Dogs	Admitted on a lead

From Brading car park, turn right out of the car park and take the road on the left, Coach Lane, at the edge of the village. At the first bend, Doctor's Lane joins from the left and the road becomes West Lane. The road bends round to the right and a few yards along it, on the left, is the entrance to Nunwell House. There has been a Nunwell House at Brading since the 11th century, the present one having its origins as a farmhouse in the 1520's. Most of this time the property has been owned by the Oglander family who kept extensive family records.

1.20   Nunwell House

Collection of family militaria; Home Guard museum; 5 acres of gardens, picnic area and shop

Location	West Lane , Brading
Operator	Colonel A.J. Aylmer
Telephone no.	407240
Opening hours	10:00 am to 5:00 pm Mon. to Wed., 1:30 pm to 5:00 pm Sunday from first Sunday in July to last Wednesday in September; closed Thurs. to Sat. Parties by arrangement throughout the year.
Admission charges	Adults £2.80, children 60p, senior citizens £2.30
Parking	In the grounds
Bus route	Southern Vectis nos. 16 & 16B to Brading
Disabled access	Wheelchair access to grounds and ground floor only
Refreshments	Tea, soft drinks and biscuits available
Toilets	Toilets in the upstairs in house, unsuitable for disabled
Dogs	On lead in grounds; guide dogs only in house

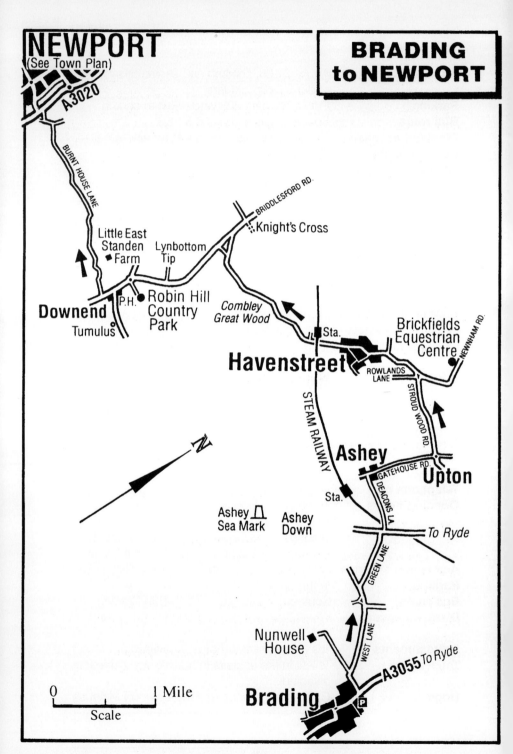

NEWPORT
(See Town Plan)

A3020

BURNT HOUSE LANE

BRIDDLESFORD RD.

Knight's Cross

Little East
Standen
Farm

Lynbottom
Tip

Downend

P.H.

Robin Hill
Country
Park

Tumulus

Combley
Great Wood

Brickfields
Equestrian
Centre

NEWNHAM RD.

Sta.

Havenstreet

ROWLANDS
LANE

STROUD WOOD RD.

STEAM RAILWAY

Ashey

GATEHOUSE RD.

Upton

DEACONS LA.

Sta.

Ashey
Sea Mark

Ashey
Down

To Ryde

GREEN LANE

WEST LANE

Nunwell
House

A3055 *To Ryde*

Brading

P

0   1 Mile

Scale

From the grounds of Nunwell House, as from most parts of east Wight, a tall black and white stone structure can be seen on the crest of Ashey Down. This is the Ashey Sea Mark, erected in 1735 to be used as a navigational aid, in conjunction with St. Helen's Church, to assist the passage of ships through St. Helen's Roads and into Brading Haven. The Corporation of Trinity House is still responsible for maintaining paintwork to ensure its visibility from the Channel and Spithead.

From Nunwell House, turn left and follow the lane to its junction with the main road from Ashey Down to Ryde. At this T-junction turn right and then take the first turning on the left towards Ashey village. Along this road, a bridge carries the road over a railway line. Don't be too startled if you encounter the steam exhaust from a train - its real, the line being part of the Havenstreet Railway. Follow the road round to the right at Ashey and up to the roundabout at Upton Cross. Turn left and go down Stroud Wood Road. Continue to the road junction with Rowlands Lane, Havenstreet Road and Newnham Lane. Turn right into Newnham Lane and proceed for a quarter of a mile to the Brickfields Horse Country.

1.21   Brickfields Horse Country

Shire horses to miniature ponies, working demonstrations; collection of carriages, vintage tractors and farm tools; working blacksmith's forge; cider making; guided tours of farm heritage; children's farm corner; children's play area; gift shop.

Location	Newnham Road, Binstead
Operator	Phillip Legge
Telephone no.	566801/615116
Opening hours	10:00 am to 5:00 pm, daily
Admission charges	Adults £3.50, children £2.50
Parking	By covered arena
Bus route	Southern Vectis no. 88 (summer only)
Disabled access	Wheelchair access
Refreshments	Restaurant, bar and picnic area on site
Toilets	On site
Dogs	Admitted on lead, except in restaurant

From the Brickfields Horse Country, return along Newnham Road towards Havenstreet, so called because it used to be the head of Wootton Creek before the causeway was built. Continue through the village, under the railway bridge and turn right into the Havenstreet Station car park.

1.22   Havenstreet Station

A working railway system, which connects with Island Line at Smallbrook Junction (10 mile round trip), using steam engines and elderly carriages; museum and shop; gardens with picnic area, children's playground and recreation field plus woodland walk. Vintage omnibus connects with trains at Wootton for round trip to Whippingham Church, Osborne House and Barton Manor.

Location	Station Road, Havenstreet
Operator	The Isle of Wight Railway Co. Ltd.
Telephone no.	884343/882204
Opening hours	Railway: Sundays only (first train 10:05 am, last train 3:05 pm) in winter; various days (see timetable; first train 10:15 am, last train 4:31 pm) in summer. Shop: 10:00 am to 5:00 pm on operating days, 10:00 am to 4:00 pm non-operating days, May to September
Admission charges	Return rail journey: Adult £4.50, children £3.50, family (2 adults and up to 4 children) £15.00
Parking	In station car park
Bus route	Southern Vectis nos. 7 & 7A; Vintage Tours hourly service between East Cowes (including Red Funnel Ferry terminal) and Wootton Station according to timetable
Disabled access	Wheelchair access to buildings and trains, plus toilet for disabled
Refreshments	Cafe: open 10:00 am to 5:00 pm on operating days; 10:30 am to 4:00 pm on non-operating days between June and September; picnic area
Toilets	By station
Dogs	Admitted

From the station, continue along the road towards Newport as far as the Briddlesford Road. Turn left up the hill past the Council waste tip. At the top of the hill is a road junction by the entrance to Robin Hill Country Park. This is basically a place of active entertainment for youngsters. However, at the eastern end of the park are the remains of a small Roman villa. This has been excavated but the site has since been covered to preserve it, so that little can be seen. It is possible to see strip lynchets, the remnants of an old field system, in the field on the south side of the copse in the park.

From the Country Park, take the road heading east from the Hare and Hounds public house. Just east of the old Downend chalk quarry, there is a damaged Bronze Age burial mound on the right, known as Michal Morey's Hump. Michal Morey, a local man, was executed at Winchester in 1737 after being found guilty of a murder at nearby Sullens Farm. His remains were subsequently displayed hanging in chains from a gibbet erected on the Bronze Age burial mound near the Hare and Hounds cross-roads. The story of his crime is recorded inside the pub.

From the Hare and Hounds, drive south for a few yards and then turn right into Burnt House Lane. This narrow lane leads along a very pleasant valley towards Newport. On the right is Little East Standen Farm. The owners were awarded a Conservation Award for rebuilding the round extension on the main barn. This type of extension housed a horse-powered drive which operated farm machinery. The horse walked in a circular track beneath a large toothed wheel. This wheel, mounted on a large vertical axle, had teeth engaging with one or more smaller geared wheels, which drove individual pieces of equipment. In this case the system would have been used to drive the machinery for threshing wheat in the main barn. It is one of the few examples of this system remaining on the Island.

At the end of Burnt House Lane, turn right on the main road, A3020, into Newport. On the left, the tall building is Pan Mill. Keep left through the Coppins Bridge roundabout system and park in the large public car park on the left, next to the mill. Walk across to the restored mill building which is now used as offices. At the rear of the building is a short flight of stairs to an observation gallery where it is possible to see some of the machinery once powered by the River Medina.

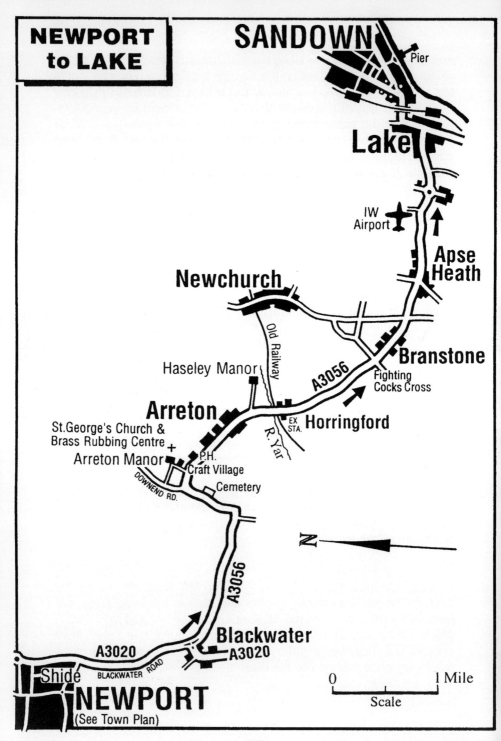

NEWPORT to LAKE

SANDOWN

Pier

Lake

IW Airport

Apse Heath

Newchurch

Old Railway

Branstone

Haseley Manor

A3056

Fighting Cocks Cross

Arreton

R. Yar

EX. STA.

Horringford

St. George's Church & Brass Rubbing Centre

Arreton Manor

DOWNEND RD.

P.H.

Craft Village

Cemetery

N

A3056

Blackwater

A3020

A3020

BLACKWATER ROAD

Shide

NEWPORT
(See Town Plan)

0   1 Mile

Scale

2. THE SOUTH-EAST FACET

Arreton — Sandown — Shanklin — Ventnor — Wroxall — Godshill — Merstone — Newport

From Newport, take the Blackwater Road towards Sandown, the A3020. The southern edge of Newport is called Shide. John Milne, the Father of Seismology, the study of earthquakes, spent the latter years of his life at Shide Hill House. He was born in Liverpool in 1850 but carried out his most important work in Japan. In 1895, he chose the Island to continue his work and he lived here until his death in 1913. The house has since been demolished.

John Milne and his Japanese wife at the entrance to Shide House, 1898. (Allan Insole)

Continue along the main A3056 road towards Arreton. The Arreton valley has been well endowed by nature with a rich soil, shelter and a good climate. For this reason it has been inhabited and cultivated since the earliest times and has a rich history. Soon after the left-hand right angle bend at Crouchers Cross is a small, isolated cemetery on the right-hand side of the road. A few hundred yards further on there is a fork in the road. Take the left-hand branch, Downend Road, which climbs up the hill to the entrance to the car park of Arreton Manor.

The manor is believed to have been left by Alfred the Great to his son Etherward. There has been a building on this site since the ninth century but it was evidently rebuilt on several occasions. The oldest rooms in the surviving manor house incorporate parts of a farmhouse built by the monks of Quarr Abbey and date from the 14th century. The present manor house is mainly Jacobean in style.

Museum of Childhood: toys and doll's houses.

Lace Museum: baby gowns, smocking and fashion accessories.

Pomeroy Museum (The National Wireless Museum): crystal sets, cat's whiskers, early wireless sets and radiograms; organises annual events such as the International Marconi Day commemoration at Puckpool Park in April and the Wight Wireless Rally at Arreton Manor in September.

Living History: For the first three weeks of May, about 30 members of The Sealed Knot and the English Civil War Society take over the old kitchens, ground floor and first floor. Throughout the day about 10 members enact life in the house as it would have been in the 16th century, while about 20 act as soldiers re-enacting battles in the copse. It is possible for parties to book Tudor period banquets at which the guests will be entertained by a juggler, musicians and players.

Gift shop and accommodation

Location	Downend Road, Arreton
Operator	Mrs J. Schroeder
Telephone no.	528134
Opening hours	10:00 am to 6:00 pm, Mondays to Fridays; 12:00 to 6:00 pm, Sundays; closed Saturdays; from one week before Easter until end of October; also visits by appointment
Admission charges	Adult £3.00, children £1.50, senior citizens £2.50
Parking	Car park off Downend Road
Bus route	Southern Vectis no. 3
Disabled access	Wheelchair access limited to ground floor
Refreshments	Tea rooms
Toilets	Near the Tea Rooms
Dogs	On a lead

Just below Arreton Manor is the 12th century church of St. George. This can be reached from Arreton Manor by a short footpath Alternatively drive down the hill and turn left to the Arreton Craft Village car park. Next to the church is a building housing the Island Brass Rubbing Centre. Incidentally, the back room of the White Lion Inn (The Cabin), adjacent to the church, houses an interesting collection of old agricultural implements.

The Centre contains replica memorial brasses from which you can make your own brass rubbings using materials provided; information on other Island brasses is provided; demonstrations of the art of brass rubbing; school parties are catered for and worksheets are available. The nearby church houses a collection of original brasses.

Location	In restored coach house next to St. George's Church, Arreton
Operator	Mrs. I. Flux
Telephone no.	402066/526290
Opening hours	9:30 am to 5:30 pm, Monday to Saturday and 2:00 pm to 5:30 pm, Sundays, Easter to October
Admission charges	Free admission but a charge is made for materials
Parking	In Arreton Craft Village car park
Bus route	Southern Vectis no. 3
Disabled access	Wheelchair access
Refreshments	In nearby Arreton Craft Village is a restaurant and ice cream kiosk
Toilets	Adjacent to centre
Dogs	Admitted on a lead

Arreton is a long village of ribbon development on both sides of the main road. After the last of the houses on the left and opposite the police station, a narrow signposted lane leads left to Haseley Manor. For almost four hundred years this manor was, like Arreton, farmed by the monks from Quarr. This is one of the oldest manor houses on the Island where you can "walk through history from medieval to Victorian times".

2.3   **Haseley Manor**

A walk through a thousand years of life at the manor house guided by a commentary, sound effects and special lighting; examples of period costumes; introduction to some of the well known characters who have lived in the house. A craft village is housed in rescued historic farm buildings. The Island's largest pottery studio with regular demonstrations where children can make an IW mouse. Sweet factory with daily demonstrations Monday to Friday.

Location	Haseley Lane, off Arreton Street
Operator	Mr. & Mrs. R. Young
Telephone no.	865420
Opening hours	10:00 am to 5:30 pm (last admission 4:00 pm), daily, Easter to end of October
Admission charges	Adults £3.65, children £2.85, senior citizens £3.10; children under 5 years old free
Parking	Car park next to the house
Bus route	Southern Vectis no. 3
Disabled access	Wheelchair access to ground floor only
Refreshments	Tea rooms in the grounds
Toilets	On site, including disabled toilets
Dogs	Admitted on a lead

Return to the main road and turn left. The road gently descends to the valley of the eastern River Yar. Immediately south of the bridge over the river (stream in reality) is Horringford railway station, now a private residence. The line of the track is still clearly visible and the section between here and Newchurch to the east along the bank of the river is a very pleasant walk. In fact you can walk along the line of the track as far as Sandown. There are several places around the Island where similar sections of old railway track provide dry, clear pathways through peaceful countryside, sometimes little changed from the days when the tracks were in use.

Continue along the main A3056 road, through Apse Heath and into Lake. At the traffic lights, turn left towards Sandown. The road passes beneath a railway bridge and through a second set of traffic lights. It then skirts the centre of Sandown before descending to a roundabout. Turn right here into Avenue Road. After quarter of a mile, a fork on the left leads into Fort Street. It is signposted to coach and car park, which are 200 yards along on the left.

From the Fort Street car park, walk down to the seafront. Turn right and walk along Culver Road for about 200 yards to the lower end of the High Street. Immediately opposite is Sandown Library with the Museum of Isle of Wight Geology on the first floor.

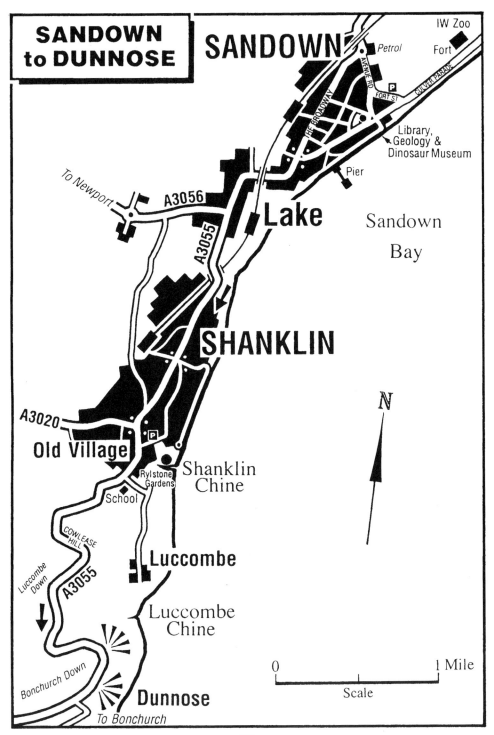

SANDOWN to DUNNOSE

SANDOWN

IW Zoo

Fort

Petrol

P

FORT ST

AVENUE RD

THE BROADWAY

CULVER PARADE

Library,
Geology &
Dinosaur Museum

Pier

To Newport

A3056

A3055

Lake

Sandown

Bay

SHANKLIN

N

A3020

Old Village

P

Rylstone
Gardens

Shanklin
Chine

School

Shanklin
Chine

COWLEASE
HILL

Luccombe
Down

A3055

Luccombe

Luccombe
Chine

Bonchurch Down

Dunnose

To Bonchurch

0   1 Mile

Scale

Walk through 120 million years of local geological history; display of dinosaurs and other fossils found on the Island; shop offering publications and gifts with a geological theme for all age groups; school parties catered for, including the organisation of fossil hunting field trips.

Location	Sandown Library, High Street
Operator	IW Council
Telephone no.	404344
Opening hours	9:30 am to 5:30 pm, Mondays to Fridays and 9:30 am to 4:30 pm Saturdays
Admission charges	Free
Parking	Fort Street public car park
Bus route	Southern Vectis nos. 2, 3, 7, 7A, 16, 16B, 20A, 22, 25, 44 & 90
Disabled access	No access for wheelchairs
Refreshments	Local cafes and restaurants
Toilets	Nearest 50 yards away, at end of Culver Road
Dogs	Not admitted

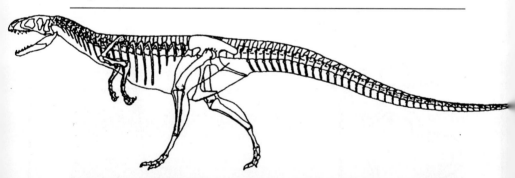

Reconstruction of a recently discovered and as yet undescribed dinosaur from the Isle of Wight. (Illustration by Steve Hutt and used with the permission of the Geological Society of the Isle of Wight)

Return along Culver Road and then continue along Culver Parade to Sandown Granite Fort which dominates the local view. This fort now forms part of the Zoological Gardens. The fort was built between 1861 and 1864 with a seaward face of granite blocks, hence the name. It was originally surrounded by a ditch but this has now been filled in. The large gun emplacements inside had iron shields to protect them from enemy fire.

Original remains of fort on view. Breeding programme of some endangered species, such as small mammals, monkeys, lemurs, reptiles and birds; specialities are big cats and snakes. Parrot, Snake and big cats shows and educational talks. Children's play area. Souvenir shop.

Location	Sandown Granite Fort, Culver Parade, Yaverland
Operator	Mr. J. Corney
Telephone no.	403883/405562
Opening hours	10am to 6pm Easter to October; 10:00 am to 5:00 pm on winter Sundays; groups by appointment on any day in the year except Dec. 25th
Admission charges	Adults £3.99, children £2.99
Parking	Public car park in front of the fort
Bus route	Southern Vectis nos. 7, 7A, 22 & 90; local "Dotto Train" in summer months
Disabled access	Access for wheelchairs
Refreshments	Snack bar on site; cafe and bar nearby
Toilets	On site
Dogs	Not admitted

General Sir William Pitt reviewing troops at Sandown on 4 June, 1798. On the left is Sandown Fort, built during the reign of Charles I. This survived until 1901, when it was demolished, the site now being beneath the tennis courts on Sandham Grounds. The structure on the right appears to have been a temporary structure built for the occasion. (Copy of engraving by Richard Livesay, 1800)

In the summer you can board the steam-powered paddle steamer *Waverley* at Sandown Pier. This makes excursions along the coast to Portsmouth, Bournemouth and Swanage. It is a reminder of earlier times when paddle steamers conveyed goods and passengers between the harbours and piers all along the south coast. If you are interested in making a sea passage and helping to support the Paddle Steamer Preservation Society at the same time contact Waverley Excursions Ltd. (tel. 01446-720656) for the timetable of sailings. A Sandown Heritage Trail leaflet is available. It may be obtained from the Tourist Information Centre located at the top of the High Street.

From the car park return along the route to the roundabout, left along the A3055 to the second set of traffic lights at Lake. Here the itinerary continues straight ahead along the A3055 into Shanklin.

Construction of Shanklin Pier began in 1888 and it was opened to steamer traffic on 18th August, 1890. This photograph shows a paddle steamer, probably the Balmoral, at the pier head in about 1910. Numerous excursion steamers visited Island piers at this time and it was possible to visit Cherbourg, Brighton, Southsea, Southampton and Bournemouth or simply go round the Island. The pier was severely damaged during the great storm of 1987 and had to be demolished. (Sylvia Taylor)

The core of Shanklin is the Old Village. This area preserves something of the hamlet as it was in the middle of the last century before the great expansion of the town. Park in the large car park on the left. From here walk down through the village to the Crab Inn. Turn left into Chine Hollow. This leads to both Shanklin Chine and Rylstone Gardens. The next exhibition is at The Swiss Chalet in Rylstone Gardens.

An exhibition set up to encourage Islanders and visitors to explore the Island and learn more about its richly varied landscape and wildlife.

Location	The Swiss Chalet, Rylstone Gardens, Shanklin
Operator	The Isle of Wight Natural History and Archaeological Society
Telephone no.	867016
Opening hours	11:00 am to 5:00 pm (last admission 4:30 pm), Monday 24th July to Sunday 3rd September (inclusive)
Admission charges	Adults £1:00, children & senior citizens 50p
Parking	Limited roadside parking; nearest public car park in Shanklin Old Village
Bus route	Southern Vectis nos. 7, 7A, 16 & 44
Disabled access	Easy access for wheelchairs
Refreshments	Cafe in the Rylstone Gardens
Toilets	Toilets (including disabled toilet) in the Rylstone Gardens
Dogs	Guide dogs only

From the car park continue along the A3055 out into open country. The road winds up Cowlease Hill and then skirts around Luccombe Down. The views along this stretch of road are magnificent on a clear day and it is worthwhile taking advantage of one of the lay-bys. Luccombe marks the eastern end of The Undercliff, the largest area of coastal landslip in western Europe. Over the centuries, landslides have produced and are still producing the distinctive terraced landscape of the area - a very large slip occurred in the winter of 1994.

Continue until a narrow road, Bonchurch Shute, branches off to the left. This lane leads down into Lower Bonchurch. An unmade track near the bottom of the Shute leads to the church of St. Boniface. This old church dates back to 1070 and has an interesting history. Return up the track and continue along Bonchurch Village Road. In the centre of the village is Bonchurch Pond, a spot favoured by artists. In fact, the whole area was a popular resort for Victorian poets, novelists and painters.

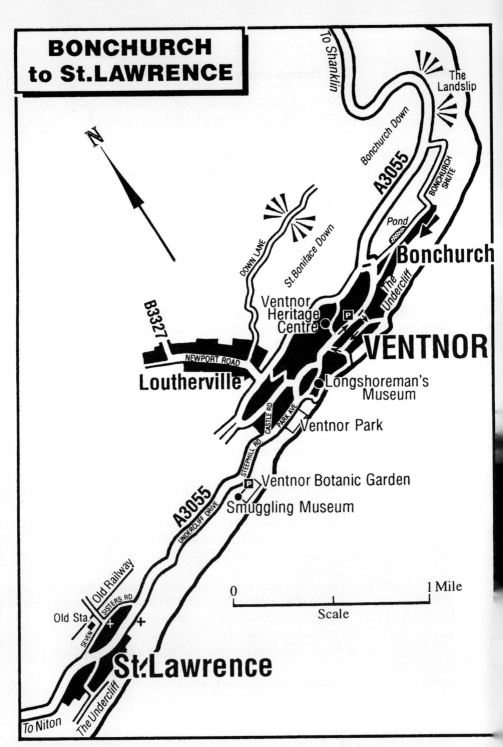

BONCHURCH to St.LAWRENCE

N

To Shanklin

The Landslip

Bonchurch Down

A3055

BONCHURCH SHUTE

Pond

St.Boniface Down

DOWN LANE

Bonchurch

The Undercliff

Ventnor Heritage Centre

B3327

NEWPORT ROAD

Loutherville

VENTNOR

Longshoreman's Museum

CASTLE RD

PARK AVE

Ventnor Park

STEEPHILL RD

Ventnor Botanic Garden

A3055

UNDERCLIFF DRIVE

Smuggling Museum

Old Railway

SISTERS RD

SEVEN

Old Sta.

St.Lawrence

To Niton

The Undercliff

0   1 Mile

Scale

Continue into Ventnor, which the Civic Trust regards as the last unspoilt Victorian seaside town in Britain. To reach the Ventnor Heritage Centre near the centre of the town, it is necessary to follow the one-way system, keeping right at the traffic lights, until you reach a car park on the left of the High Street.

2.7	**Ventnor Heritage Museum**

Artefacts, photographs and articles relating to the history of the Undercliff from Luccombe to Blackgang; numerous publications on aspects of local heritage on sale; reference library and card catalogue available by appointment

Location	11 Spring Hill, Ventnor (off the High Street)
Operator	Ventnor and District Local History Society
Telephone no.	855407
Opening hours	10:00 am to 12:30 pm and 2:00 pm to 4:30 pm, every weekday, except Wed and Sat afternoons, April to November
Admission charges	40p, senior citizens 20p
Parking	In nearby High Street public car park
Bus route	Southern Vectis nos. 2A, 7, 7A, 16, 16B & 31
Disabled access	Difficult access for wheelchairs
Refreshments	Local cafes and restaurants
Toilets	In Market Street, across the High Street
Dogs	On a lead

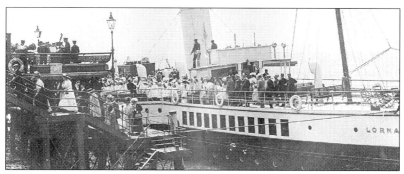

The PS Lorna Doone at Ventnor Pier in about 1910. The building of this pier began in 1871 but it was not completed until 1887. This photograph gives an impression of the large numbers of people were brought to the Island by excursion steamers in the years before the First World War. (Sylvia Taylor)

Ventnor Esplanade and beach from the pier about 1890. Ventnor developed rapidly from a small fishing village to a seaside town after the Undercliff was described as 'a highly favourable residence for invalids throughout the year' by the eminent physician Sir James Clark in 1829. The numerous bathing machines on the beach were only for use by women. (Allan Insole)

From the Heritage Museum, walk down the High Street, then left down Pier Street to reach the Esplanade. Half way along the Esplanade is the Longshoreman's Museum.

2.8 Longshoreman's Museum

Seafaring and local history of Ventnor and the Undercliff; colourful displays with model boats etc.; artefacts, engravings and photographs of the Victorian era.

Location	The Esplanade, Ventnor
Operator	Mr. & Mrs. Blake
Telephone no.	853176
Opening hours	9:30 am to 4:00 pm, daily, Easter to Christmas
Admission charges	Adults 50p, children (8-14) 25p
Parking	At end of Esplanade
Bus route	Southern Vectis nos. 2A, 7, 7A, 16, 16B & 31
Disabled access	Access for wheelchairs
Refreshments	Adjacent cafes, restaurant and public houses
Toilets	At both ends of Esplanade
Dogs	On a lead

From the car park, follow the one-way system round to the traffic lights and turn left. This is the A3055 which takes you towards Niton. Very soon the road passes Ventnor Park on the left with an example of a Victorian bandstand. Shortly after passing a caravan site and cricket ground on the left, the entrance to Ventnor Botanic Gardens is reached. Park at the far end of the car park in the grounds.

The Royal National Hospital was built between 1868 and 1897 as a centre for the cure of chest complaints, particularly tuberculosis. With the introduction of an effective chemical treatment for tuberculosis in the late 1940's, the hospital began to run down. The hospital was finally closed in 1964 and demolished in 1969, the site now being the car park for the Ventnor Botanic Gardens which occupy the former grounds of the hospital. (George Hook)

The gardens occupy the site of the Royal National Hospital for Diseases of the Chest. The hospital was founded here in 1868 beneath the high southern Downs to take advantage of the local microclimate which alleviated the symptoms of several chest complaints, especially tuberculosis. Advances in antibiotics made the huge hospital redundant and in the 1960's it was demolished. The grounds were turned into public botanic gardens. Taking full advantage of the mild climate, the gardens are used to grow over 3,500 species of the world's trees, shrubs and plants, including Mediterranean and New Zealand collections. Special displays are housed in a Temperate House. A picnic area and adventure playground for children is located at the west end of the grounds beyond the Temperate House.

Magnificent collection of herbaceous plants, shrubs and trees, many of which grow here because of the unusual microclimate of the Undercliff. In the foyer of the Temperate House is a small exhibition showing the history of the Royal National Hospital for Diseases of the Chest. An unusual feature is the collection of medicinal plants in the grounds, developed using funds donated by the local branch of the Royal Pharmaceutical Society.

Location	Steephill Road, Ventnor
Operator	IW Council
Telephone no.	855397
Opening hours	**Gardens**: 9:00 am to dusk in winter; 9:00 am to 10:00pm in summer
	Temperate House: 10:00 am to 4:00 pm on winter Sundays; 10:00 am to 4:00 pm, daily, Easter to September; 10:00 am to 4:30 pm in summer
Admission charges	Free except for entrance to Temperate House for which there is a small charge of 50p for adults and 20p for children
Parking	In the grounds
Bus route	Southern Vectis nos. 7, 7A, 16 & 31
Disabled access	Access for wheelchairs
Refreshments	The Garden Tavern, licensed tea rooms in the grounds
Toilets	In the car park near entrance to the Smugglers Museum
Dogs	Admitted on a lead to gardens, but not in Temperate House

At the western end of the car park, tucked under a sheltering wall, is a small building. This contains the entrance to the Museum of Smuggling History which is housed in vaults below the car park.

Descend into the vaults and cellars to see documents and life-size tableaux explaining smuggling techniques and the personalities involved since the 13th century from wool smugglers to contemporary drug traffickers.

Location	Ventnor Botanic Gardens car park, Steephill Road
Operator	Mr. R. Dowling
Telephone no.	853677
Opening hours	10:00 am to 5:00 pm, daily, Easter to end of September
Admission charges	Adults £1.50, children and senior citizens 90p
Parking	Botanic Gardens car park
Bus route	Southern Vectis nos. 7, 7A, 16 & 31
Disabled access	No access for wheelchairs
Refreshments	The Garden Tavern, licensed tea rooms in the Botanic Gardens grounds
Toilets	By entrance to museum
Dogs	Not admitted

From the car park, turn left onto the main A3055 road. At this point it is called Undercliff Drive. Proceed for three quarters of a mile and take the fourth turning on your right, Seven Sisters Road. A short distance up this road on the left is the Church of St. Lawrence, the smallest church on the Island with a seating capacity of less than 50. The church largely escaped Victorian restoration and surprisingly still has Georgian wooden hat pegs on its walls. A short distance further up the road, on the right, is the old St. Lawrence station, now a private house. This was on the Merstone Junction to Ventnor West railway line which opened in 1900 and closed in 1952.

Return to Undercliff Drive and turn left, back along to Steephill Road. Just beyond the Botanic Gardens, fork left up Castle Road. The name of the road refers to Steephill Castle, a mock-Gothic residence built here in 1833. Unfortunately, it no longer exists. At the top of the road, turn sharp left into Lower Gillscliff Road and then sharp right into Upper Gillscliff Road. This climbs up to the junction with the main B3327 road. Turn left towards Newport.

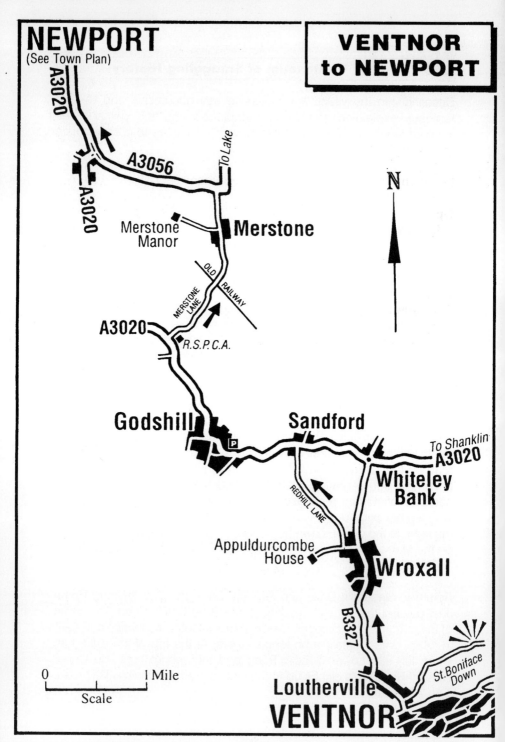

NEWPORT
(See Town Plan)

A3020

A3056

A3020

To Lake

Merstone
Manor

Merstone

VENTNOR
to NEWPORT

N

OLD RAILWAY

MERSTONE LANE

A3020

R.S.P.C.A.

Godshill

Sandford

To Shanklin
A3020

Whiteley
Bank

REDHILL LANE

Appuldurcombe
House

Wroxall

B3327

St. Boniface
Down

0   1 Mile
Scale

Loutherville
VENTNOR

Steephill Castle, a castellated mock-Gothic mansion, was built in 1833 by John Hambrough. In the 1870's, the Empress of Austria and Empress Eugénie stayed here. Later it was purchased by John Morgan Richards, an American businessman and father of Mrs. Pearl Craigie, who wrote under the pseudonym of "John Oliver Hobbs". The Castle was pulled down in 1964. (George Hook).

At this point, if the weather is fine it is worth taking a slight detour. At the crest of the hill, turn right into Down Lane. This narrow lane leads up to the top of Boniface Down. This is the highest point on the Island. It was the site of an important radar station during the Second World War. It is now the location of Ventnor Air Traffic Control. The views from the top of the Down are magnificent. There is an extensive system of easily walked paths across the area.

Return to the Newport Road and turn right towards Wroxall. On the far side of the village, a narrow lane, Appuldurcombe Road, leads off to the left. This leads to the car park of Appuldurcombe House, the remains of a once fine 18th century house built in the short-lived English Baroque style. It stands amidst rolling green countryside in its own ornamental grounds landscaped by "Capability" Brown. It was originally the seat of the Worsley family but they sold the estate in 1855. The house then passed through a succession of owners. After 1909 it was unoccupied, except for troops during the two world wars. In the Second World War, a landmine exploded close by and this destroyed the roof and windows of the building leaving the shell of the original building. Part of the roof has recently been restored.

Appuldurcombe House was built in two main phases: the first by Sir Robert Worsley 1701-13 and the second by Sir Richard Worsley 1773-82. It was the only house to be built in the grand manner on the Island. This photograph shows the east front of the house in 1912, some three years after it had become uninhabited. The once beautiful house gradually deteriorated until 1952 when it came into the care of what is now English Heritage. (Allan Insole)

2.11   Appuldurcombe House

There is a small museum in the lodge giving the full history of the house; extensive attractive grounds. The Freemantle Gate, the old entrance, lies 3/4 mile away across the grounds.

Location	At the end of Appuldurcombe Road, west of Wroxall
Operator	English Heritage
Telephone no.	852484
Opening hours	10:00 am to 6:00 pm, daily, 1st April to 30th September
Admission charges	Adults £1.20, children 60p, senior citizens 90p; free to English Heritage members
Parking	At beginning of path to the house
Bus route	Southern Vectis nos. 2A & 16B
Disabled access	Access for wheelchairs but there is a mile long uphill walk from the car park
Refreshments	None
Toilets	In the grounds
Dogs	Allowed on leads

A short distance back down Appuldurcombe Road, take Redhill Lane on the left. This leads to the main A3020 Shanklin - Newport road at Sandford. Turn left and follow the main road into Godshill. This village is famed for its "chocolate box" view of the church on the hill, framed by thatched cottages. It became a tourist attraction when local transport became easily available. Facilities for the visitor have developed over the years but the village still retains its fascinating aura of the 1930's with its thatched tea rooms and model village. For an experience in contrasts, visit both the parish church on the hill and the Methodist Chapel near the car park at the eastern end of the village.

From Godshill, continue towards Newport. About half a mile beyond the village, Merstone Lane branches off to the right. Take this and continue for a mile to the village of Merstone. On the way you cross a section of the old IW Central Railway with remains of the platform of Merstone Station on the left. In Merstone, take Chapel Lane on the left, which leads to Merstone Manor, not open to the public. This is a brick-built Jacobean building with stone additions. The manor is mentioned in the Domesday Book. The open aspect of the property allows the passer-by to appreciate a fine example of the many manor houses with which the Island is endowed. Return to Merstone Village. Turn left up the narrow lane to the main road and left again. This is the main A3056 Lake-Newport road which leads directly back to Newport.

3. THE SOUTH-WEST FACET

Carisbrooke — Chale — Shorwell — Brighstone — Brook — Freshwater — Totland — Calbourne — Newport

From Newport, take the Carisbrooke Road. At the end of the section with raised pavements, known locally as The Mall, is a triangular patch of grass with a prominent war memorial standing on it. Fork left here and proceed up Castle Road. At the roundabout, turn right (not sharp right) into Castle Hill and up to Carisbrooke Castle. A traffic light controls traffic flow round one of the fortifying buttresses of Carisbrooke Castle. This arrowhead buttress has been unaltered since it was built between 1597 and 1601. From the car park at the end of the road, it is easy to appreciate why this site was chosen for a castle. The castle dates from the Norman era but was modified many times. The chief claim to fame

Carisbrooke Castle. has stood for nearly a thousand years. During this time it was besieged by King Stephen in the 12th century, attacked by the French on several occasions during the 14th century and acted as a prison for King Charles I between 1647 and 1648. By late Victorian times, when this photograph was taken, it had become a tourist attraction and a regular horse bus service ran between Newport and the castle. (Allan Insole)

of the castle is that it was used to imprison Charles I from 1647 to 1648. More recently, Princess Beatrice, the youngest daughter of Queen Victoria lived in the Governor's House from 1913 to 1939.

3.1	Carisbrooke Castle

Seven acres of castle, buildings and earthworks to explore; battlements and keep give splendid views over the surrounding area; donkeys work the 16th century wheel to pull water from the well; shop with stock of books, gifts and souvenirs.

The Governor's House contains the independent **Carisbrooke Castle Museum** which exhibits the history of both the Island and the castle; the lower gallery has some Stuart relics and various objects relating to the castle; the upper gallery has a fine 1602 chamber organ and some Tennyson memorabilia; personal stereo tour at an additional charge; souvenir shop.

Location	Castle Hill, Carisbrooke
Operator	English Heritage
Telephone no.	Carisbrooke Castle (English Heritage) 522107; Carisbrooke Castle Museum 523112
Opening hours	10:00 am to 6:00 pm, daily, 1st April to 30th Sept.; 10:00 am to 4:00 pm, daily, 1st Oct. to 31st March; closed 24th to 26th Dec.
Admission charges	Adults £3.20, children £1.60, senior citizens £2.40; free to English Heritage members
Parking	Public car park
Bus route	Southern Vectis nos. 16B, 31 & 36 (bottom of Castle Hill)
Disabled access	Wheelchair access to grounds and lower levels of structure only
Refreshments	Cafe outside the gate, summer only
Toilets	In the grounds
Dogs	On a lead

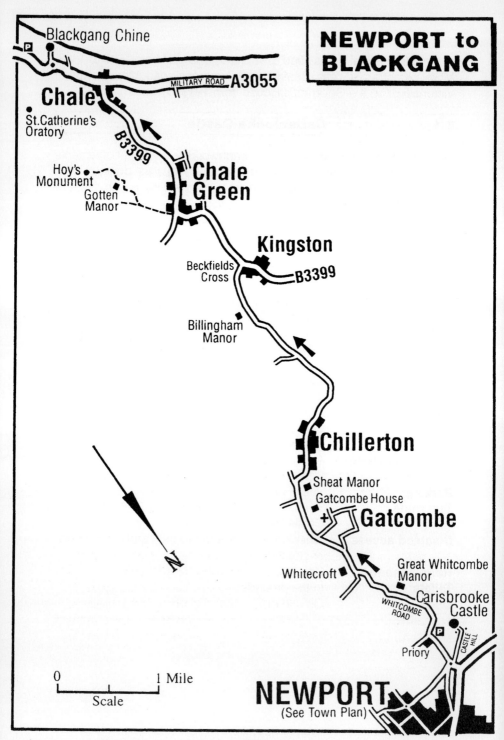

NEWPORT to BLACKGANG

Blackgang Chine

MILITARY ROAD A3055

Chale

St.Catherine's Oratory

B3399

Hoy's Monument

Gotten Manor

Chale Green

Kingston

Beckfields Cross

B3399

Billingham Manor

N

Chillerton

Sheat Manor

Gatcombe House

Gatcombe

Whitecroft

Great Whitcombe Manor

WHITCOMBE ROAD

Carisbrooke Castle

CASTLE HILL

Priory

NEWPORT
(See Town Plan)

0   1 Mile
Scale

Return to the roundabout at the bottom of Castle Hill and turn right up the Whitcombe Road. At the top of the hill, by the car park overlooking the castle, there is a building on the left which was, until recently, a Dominican Priory. Further along the valley are the manors of Great Whitcombe, Gatcombe and Sheat. At the time of the Domesday survey, there was a single manorial estate in this part of the Medina valley, known as Gatcombe. Subsequently this was divided into the three smaller manors, although they remained in the hands of a single family. Hence the name of the southernmost, Sheat, which is derived from "scest", meaning a parcel or slice of a manor.

The first, Great Whitcombe House, lies on the right, half a mile beyond the car park. It has impressive views over the valley to the east. A further half a mile on, the campanile of Whitecroft Hospital can be seen over the trees to the left. This was built in 1896 as the Island's lunatic asylum, but now other uses are being found for the extensive buildings.

Half a mile beyond the Whitecroft junction is the signposted turning on the right to Gatcombe Church along Gatcombe Road. Gatcombe was owned by the Seely family in the early twentieth century and Sir Charles did a lot to maintain this beautiful church. When his son died at Gaza in 1917, he had a memorial created in the form of a medieval knight's tomb. From the church return to the main road. The impressive Georgian manor house lies on the right, set well back from the road. It was built in 1751 by Edward Worsley.

Sheat Manor lies about half a mile south of Gatcombe. It is a fine example of a stone-built Jacobean manor house. Unfortunately it is difficult to view this house from the main road as it lies on a double bend.

The road continues through Chillerton towards Chale Green. About one and a half miles beyond Chillerton, on the left hand side of the road, is a fourth manor house, Billingham Manor. At the time of the Domesday Book, this was part of the very large Bowcombe manorial estate and was held by the King. The presence of so many manor houses in the upper Medina valley attests to the fertility and productivity of the land in this part of the Island.

Beyond Billingham Manor, at Beckfield Cross, the road joins the B3399. Continue along this towards Chale Green. At the Y-junction on the northern outskirts of Chale Green, a steep footpath (C1) leads up to the Hoy Monument on top of St. Catherine's Down. About a quarter of a mile along the path, just below a copse, the path divides. The right hand path leads past Gotten Manor Farm. There is an early stone building, with an external flight of stone steps to the upper storey. A later 17th century house adjoins it. The name Gotten could be from the Norman Godeton family, or the Domesday name Gadetune. Michael Hoy, who lived here in the early 19th Century built the monument on top of the hill, to record the visit of the Tsar of Russia to England in 1814. In 1857, his successor added a commemoration to those who died in the Crimean War.

Continue from Chale Green to Chale. On the left on the northern edge of the village, it is possible to see Chale Abbey Farm. Despite its church-like window, this was not a church, having a north - south orientation. It is a contender for the oldest continuously occupied house on the Island.

At the junction with the Military Road (A3055), south of Chale, turn left up to the viewpoint car park above Blackgang. On a clear day the view from here is remarkable. It is possible to see the whole of the south-western coast of the Island along to the Needles and the coast of Dorset beyond. It is worthwhile walking a short distance along the clifftop path that leads out of the car park. From the top of the cliff, the path overlooks the area affected by large scale landslips.

On the opposite side of the main road to the car park, a steep path ascends to the top of Niton Down. Here there stand two early light houses. The first, known locally as the Pepperpot, is the remaining tower of a 14th century oratory. In 1313 a vessel carrying wine from Bordeaux was wrecked in Chale Bay. Some of the wine was recovered and found its way into the hands of the local lord of the manor, Walter de Godeton. Unfortunately for Walter, the wine had been bound for a religious house. Walter was brought before an ecclesiastical court and, as a penance, had to build an oratory on the hill above Chale Bay. He also had to pay for a monk to tend a light in the oratory tower and to say prayers for the dead seafarers. The light was tended until the Dissolution of the Monasteries in the time of Henry VIII. Later, because of the dangers to shipping along this part of the Island's coast, Trinity House tried to build a lighthouse close by. Only the base was ever built. It was realised that the top of the Down was frequently shrouded in mist and this would have made the light useless. Trinity House then built St. Catherine's Lighthouse on the coast below Niton.

From the viewpoint car park, return down the hill and into the large car park at Blackgang Chine. It is often said that Blackgang derives its name from a smuggling gang known as "The Black Gang" that was supposed to have operated in the vicinity at one time. In practice, it probably derives from "black", a reference to the dark cliffs, and "gang", meaning a "way" since, until the end of the last century, there used to be a path down to the beach here. A chine is derived from a Saxon word meaning "cleft" or "ravine". Today, the name Blackgang Chine is synonymous with an adventure centre for youngsters, featuring such attractions as Frontierland, Nurseryland and Fantasyland. However, there are also two heritage exhibitions.

By the time the late 19th century, Blackgang Chine had become a tourist attraction. In the 1880's, when this photograph was taken, it was still possible to walk down through the chine to the beach. Rapid coastal erosion along this stretch of the coast soon made this impossible. (Allan Insole)

3.2 Blackgang Theme Park, Timberworld and St. Catherine's Quay

Timberworld is based around a water powered sawmill with displays of the uses of wood, include the wheelwright, the cooper and the carpenter; also working engines and domestic scenes circa 1890; animated figures and commentary bring these and other displays to life. Outside there is a reconstructed quayside complete with an old Island lifeboat. Shop with instructive books and souvenirs.

Location	Blythe Shute, Chale
Operator	Messrs. Dabell
Telephone no.	730330/730305
Opening hours	10:00 am to 5:00 pm, daily from 28th March to 28th Sept.; 10:00 am to 6:00 pm, daily from 21st to 27th March and from 29th Sept to 30th Oct; 10:00 am to 4:00 pm, daily for remainder of year
Admission charges	Adults £2.25, children £1.75
Parking	Large public car park adjacent to exhibition
Bus route	Southern Vectis nos. 7, 7A, 16B & 31
Disabled access	Not suitable for wheelchairs
Refreshments	Cafe on site
Toilets	On site
Dogs	Not admitted

From Blackgang descend via the A3055 to the area known as "The Back of the Wight". Originally there was no road along the south-west coast of the Island. In the mid-19th century, a road was built by the government to connect Freshwater to Chale. The aim was to allow the military garrison at Freshwater to rapidly reach any enemy landing along this stretch of coast. Hence, it became known as the Military Road. Traces of the original military fence still exist along some sections of the road. In the 1930's the road was improved through a government scheme to provide work for the unemployed. It is believed that some of the workers were unemployed miners from Wales. When completed, the road was opened to the public with the Prince of Wales being driven along it.

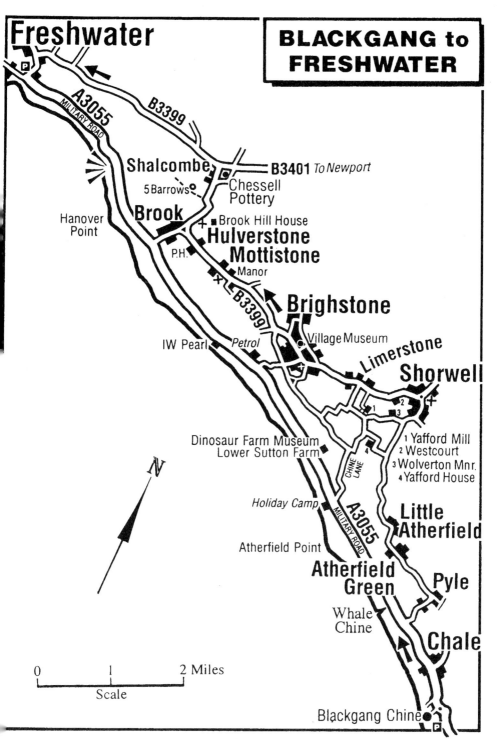

Freshwater

BLACKGANG to FRESHWATER

A3055 MILITARY ROAD

B3399

Shalcombe

5 Barrows

Brook

Chessell Pottery

B3401 *To Newport*

Hanover Point

Brook Hill House

P.H.

Hulverstone
Mottistone

Manor

B3399

Brighstone

IW Pearl

Petrol

Village Museum

Limerstone

Shorwell

2
1
3
+

Dinosaur Farm Museum
Lower Sutton Farm

1 Yafford Mill
2 Westcourt
3 Wolverton Mnr.
4 Yafford House

CHINE LANE

4

Little
Atherfield

Holiday Camp

A3055 MILITARY ROAD

N

Atherfield Point

Atherfield
Green

Pyle

Whale
Chine

Chale

0   1   2 Miles
Scale

Blackgang Chine

One mile west of Chale, there is a large lay-by beside the road on the left. If you stop here and follow the coastal footpath, SW30, towards the coast, it leads to Whale Chine. This is a miniature Grand Canyon cut into the cliffs of Chale Bay. It gets its name from a large whale that was stranded here many years ago.

Continue along the A3055 for about two miles. Here a track on the right leads to Lower Sutton Farm and the Dinosaur Farm Museum.

3.3	Dinosaur Farm Museum

The skeleton of a very large dinosaur, found locally, is being extracted from the rock and prepared for exhibition. The public are invited to watch the work as it proceeds; other local fossils on display; fossil identification service; fossil walks (by appointment).

Location	Lower Sutton Farm, Brighstone
Operator	Mr. & Mrs. J. Phillips
Telephone no.	740401/01374-712697
Opening hours	10:00 am to 5:00 pm, Thursdays and Sundays from 13th April to 28th Sept.; also Tuesday in July and August; coaches by appointment
Admission charges	Adults £1.50, children £0.75, senior citizens £1.00
Parking	Public car park adjacent to exhibition
Bus route	Southern Vectis nos. 7 & 7A
Disabled access	Access for wheelchairs
Refreshments	None but picnic tables provided
Toilets	On site
Dogs	Admitted on a lead

Cutting hay with scythes, Shanklin, about 1880. Although mechanical mowers were introduced in the 1850's, scythes continued to be used well into this century. A good scytheman could cut about an acre of hay in a day. (Allan Insole)

From Lower Sutton Farm, return along the A3055 to Atherfield Holiday Camp, then turn left into Chine Lane. At the junction with Thorness Lane, turn right and then take the first on the left, Mill Lane. This leads to Yafford Mill.

3.4 Yafford Mill

Restored and working 18th century water mill; agricultural museum with steam engine and antique farm machinery; examples of rare breeds of sheep, cattle and goats; ornamental waterfowl and trout pond; narrow gauge railway; guided tours and nature trail; playground, picnic area and gift shop.

Location	Mill Lane Yafford (alternative access is off the Limerstone Road, between Shorwell and Brighstone)
Operator	Penny & David Coates
Telephone no.	740610
Opening hours	10:00 am to 6:00 pm daily
Admission charges	Adults £2.20, children and senior citizens £1.40
Parking	Next to mill
Bus route	Southern Vectis nos. 7B
Disabled access	Wheelchair access to ground floor only
Refreshments	Tea Garden and Licensed Bar
Toilets	On site
Dogs	On a lead

From the Mill, return along Mill Lane for a few hundred yards, then turn left into Wolverton Lane. A quarter of a mile along this road is a right-angled, right hand bend. Stop at this bend and look left. From here there is a good view of Wolverton Manor. This house was rebuilt in the reign of Elizabeth I in a typical E-shaped groundplan. Continue along the lane into Shorwell. Turn left at the roundabout by the church into Walkers Lane (B3399). On the right is the Crown Inn. Shorwell is a very attractive village with a row of thatched cottages and a manor house, North Court, beyond the church. The church is one of the few on the Island with a five bell peal. Continue along Walkers Lane, passing West Court Farm on the left. This is another beautiful Elizabethan manor house. The road now becomes Limerstone Road and leads to Brighstone village.

Building a hayrick, near Newport in about 1905. Once the hay had been dried in the meadow, it was gathered and carted to the rick. On the right is completed stack, complete with thatched top. The rick was a store of winter feed for cattle. (George Hook)

A preserved traction engine operating a threshing machine at Gotten Manor Farm, Chale in 1970. In the 19th century, before the advent of the petrol engine, the only sources of power available on the farm were horses and steam engines. (Roger Smith)

Park by the shops on the left. Alternatively there is a public car park down the small lane on the left, just past the shops. Cross the main road into a lane called North Street. Here there is a National Trust shop. Next to it, in a National Trust cottage, is the Brighstone Village Museum.

3.5   Brighstone Village Museum

Exhibition of photographs, documents and artefacts showing the history of the village, rural life in Victorian times and in wartime and peace through the ages. Connected to the National Trust shop which has informative books, souvenirs and gifts for sale.

Location   The Old Post Office, North Street
Operator   Brighstone Village Museum Trust
Telephone no.   740843
Opening hours   Same times as National Trust shop, normally
                        9:00 am to 5:00 pm daily
Admission charges   Free
Parking   Roadside parking by shops in Main Road or in
                        village car park in Warne's Lane
Bus route   Southern Vectis no. 7B
Disabled access   Access for wheelchairs into the museum is easy
                        but the normal exit is through the National Trust
                        shop and there is a high step down into the
                        shop; a portable ramp may be available but
                        there is limited space within the shop
Refreshments   Brighstone Tea Gardens in Main Road
Toilets   In village car park in Warne's Lane
Dogs   Guide dogs only

From Brighstone continue along the main road, B3399, for a mile and a half until Mottistone Church is seen on the left. A few yards further, on the right a track leads into a National Trust Car Park. Mottistone Manor lies opposite the church. The manor is pre-Norman in origin and has always been an important one. After the Norman Conquest, it was owned by the de Insulas family. The oldest part of the present house, the east wing, was built in the 15th century by the Cheke family. In 1567, Thomas Cheke added the west wing. The manor later past through a number of hands. In 1706, there was a landslide which engulfed the rear of the east wing. The strong building itself was undamaged and the soil was left where it rested. The house was purchased by the Seely family in 1861. In 1926 Jack Seely moved his family from Brook House to Mottistone and he became the first Lord Mottistone. Under the supervision of his architect son, John, the soil was removed and renovation work was carried out leaving the building as you see it today. It is now owned by the National Trust. The gardens are open between 2:00 pm and 5:30 pm on Wednesday afternoons and Bank Holiday Mondays from 2nd March to 28th September. There is an entrance fee of £1.80. The church gate has an unusual entrance, possibly designed to ease the handling of coffins into the churchyard.

The most interesting feature in the Mottistone area can be found at the top of Castle Hill, above the hamlet. It can be reached by a path, BS43, which starts at the eastern end of the car park. A board in the car park displays a map and information. At the top of the path is a standing stone known as the Longstone. The Longstone is accompanied by a second large stone which lies beside it. These two stones are the most obvious traces of a Neolithic long barrow - the low mound of which can be seen to the west of the Longstone - built about 3000 B.C. This is one of only three Neolithic long barrows known on the Island. The two stones might be either the ritual markers at the wide eastern end of the barrow or possibly the remains of a burial chamber. Mottistone means "the stone of the speaker" in Old English. This implies that the Longstone was a meeting place in Anglo-Saxon times. On a fine day the view from the top of Castle Hill makes the climb worthwhile. Below is the coast where so many sailing ships were wrecked. The Brook and Brighstone Lifeboats, launched in Brook Bay from horsedrawn carts and rowed out through the surf, carried out many daring rescues. .

Brook lifeboat Susan Ashley being hauled up Brook Chine by horses. At one time the dangerous coast between the Needles and St. Catherine's Point possessed lifeboat stations at Atherfield, Brighstone and Brook. The Susan Ashley remained on service at Brook from 1907 to 1937, when the station was closed. The shell of the lifeboat house can still be seen at the top of Brook Chine, a reminder of the bravery of local lifeboatmen. (Sylvia Taylor)

From Mottistone, continue along the main road through Hulverstone. At the next junction fork right. Opposite the junction is Brook House. Henry VII stayed here in 1499. In 1850 it became the first Island home of Charles Seely. His grandson Jack Seely became the first Lord Mottistone. Over the years the Seely family have contributed generously to the Subscription Fund of the RNLI and Jack Seely was a crew member, coxswain and supporter for forty years.

From the junction, the road climbs up to Brook Down. At the top of the hill, stop in the small parking area on the left. From here a footpath, BS53, leads along the down which is owned by the National Trust. After about three hundred yards, it is possible to climb up to the crest of the down where there are five Bronze Age barrows. These burial mounds were built over a long period of time and several different shapes can be seen, bowl, bell and disc. It is not difficult to realise why this site, with its magnificent views of the west Wight, was chosen as a burial site. 4,500 years ago, when the barrows were built, the view would have been very different from what we see today. Currently, the coastline in this area is eroding at the rate of between 3 and 6 feet per year. A rough calculation suggests that, in Bronze Age times, the coast lay as much as two miles further south than it is today. For local farmers, this rate of erosion is a serious problem, but for local geologists it is a blessing because it continually reveals bones of dinosaurs and other fossil animals and plants which are buried in the cliffs hereabouts. On the walk back to the car park, Brook Hill House can be seen ahead. This was built in Edwardian times. J.B. Priestly, the author and playwright, lived here for several years.

From Brook Down, the road descends into Shalcombe. In the woods on the right hand side of the road, a Jutish burial ground was found and excavated in the last century. The pottery and other grave goods found provided evidence of the early Anglo-Saxon settlement of the area. Further down the hill is a pond on the left and, in the trees beyond, Shalcombe Manor. In the Domesday Book, Shalcombe is listed as belonging to the church of St. Nicholas-in-the-Castle, Carisbrooke. Soon after the foundation of Quarr Abbey in 1132, the various endowments of the chapel of St. Nicholas, including Shalcombe, were granted to Quarr. The monks established a grange here which remained their property until the abbey was dissolved in 1536.

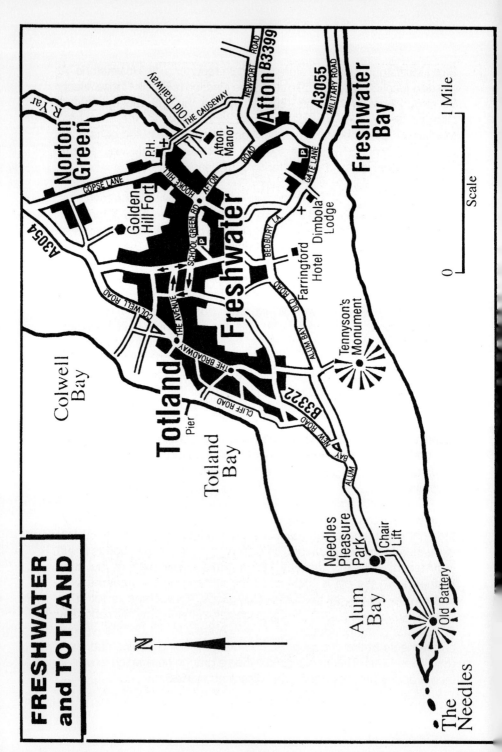

FRESHWATER and TOTLAND

N

The Needles

Old Battery

Alum Bay

Chair Lift

Needles Pleasure Park

Colwell Bay

Totland

Pier

Totland Bay

CLIFF ROAD

NEW ROAD

ALUM BAY

B3322

THE BROADWAY

THE AVENUE

COLWELL ROAD

A3054

COPSE LANE

Norton Green

R. Yar

THE CAUSEWAY

Old Railway

P.H.

HOOK HILL

Golden Hill Fort

SCHOOL GREEN RD.

AFTON ROAD

Afton Manor

NEWPORT ROAD

Afton B3399

A3055

MILITARY ROAD

Freshwater Bay

GATE LANE

Dimbola Lodge

Farringford Hotel

BEDBURY LA.

ALUM BAY OLD ROAD

Freshwater

Tennyson's Monument

Scale

0   1 Mile

The Third Isle of Wight Pop Festival held at East Afton Farm, Freshwater over the August Bank Holiday in 1970 is estimated to have attracted as many as 300,000 fans. They were entertained by some of the famous names of the time, including Joan Baez, Jimmy Hendrix, The Who and The Doors. (Eric Toogood)

At the junction with the B3401 Newport-Freshwater road, turn left towards Freshwater. Continue along this road for about three miles. Afton Down on the south of the road was the site of the famous Isle of Wight Pop Festival in 1970. At the T-junction with Afton Road, turn left and proceed to Freshwater Bay. At the next junction by a car park, turn right into Gate Lane. A quarter of a mile further on, turn into Terrace Lane on the left and park in the car park of Dimbola Lodge.

Strong winds and a high tide drove the Carl ashore in Freshwater Bay on November 5th , 1916, fortunately without any loss of life. A channel was later blasted through the offshore rock bar and the ship was able to be recovered. (Eric Toogood)

3.6   Dimbola Lodge

The building is being restored to its original condition when it was the home and workplace of Julia Margaret Cameron, the pioneer Victorian photographer. On the ground floor is the tea room which also houses a collection of historic cameras. On the first floor is an annotated collection of her photographs of Island residents and famous visitors. There is also a shop selling books and prints, an art gallery and craft shop. *No smoking allowed in the building.*

Location	Terrace Lane, Freshwater Bay
Operator	Julia Margaret Cameron Trust
Telephone no.	756814
Opening hours	10:00 am to 5:00 pm, Tuesday to Sunday
Admission charges	Adults £ 1.00, free to members of the JMC Trust and children
Parking	In front of the house or in the public car parks in the bay
Bus route	Southern Vectis nos. 7, 7A, 7B & 7C
Disabled access	There are three steps up to the ground floor and currently there is no disabled access to the gallery upstairs
Refreshments	Victorian Tea Room
Toilets	In the house
Dogs	Not admitted

Leaving Terrace Lane, turn left and continue along Gate Lane towards Totland. St. Agnes church, on the left, is a rare thatched church. Although it looks old, it is in fact relatively new, being built as recently as 1908 on land donated by Lord Tennyson's son. Further on, on the left, is Farringford Hotel, one time home of Lord Tennyson. This is open to the public for refreshments and accommodation, with the added attraction of being able to see Tennyson's Library where he wrote some of his famous works.

From the entrance to the hotel continue along Bedbury Lane and then the Alum Bay Old Road, known as Moon's Hill. After a mile and a half, there is a junction with the wider Alum Bay New Road. Turn left to reach the Needles Pleasure Park. Since no public vehicles are allowed beyond this point, it is necessary to park in the public car park here for a fee of £1.50. It is possible to walk the mile along the coastal path overlooking Alum Bay to reach the Needles Old Battery. Alternatively, there is a half hourly bus in the summer season.

3.7   Needles Old Battery

A Victorian fort built between 1862 and 1863, 77 metres above sea level with a 60 metre tunnel leading to spectacular views of the Needles, the lighthouse and, on a fine day, the Hampshire and Dorset coastline; two original rifled muzzle loader gun barrels are mounted on carriages in the parade ground; restored laboratory, searchlight position and position finding cells; an exhibition tells the story of "The Needles at War" and there are cartoon information boards throughout. Shop selling pamphlets giving the history of the Battery is open at the same times as the battery, except closed between 2 and 13 October.

Location	West High Down
Operator	The National Trust
Telephone no.	523831
Opening hours	10:30 am to 5:00 pm (last admission 4.30pm), daily , Easter Weekend and the whole of July & August; Sunday to Thursday only between 27th March and June 30th and between 1st Sept and 30th Oct
Admission charges	Adults £2.40, children £1.20; free to National Trust members
Parking	In the Needles Pleasure Park car park (charge £1.50)
Bus route	Southern Vectis nos. 7, 7A, 7B, 7C & 42
Disabled access	Not recommended for visitors with disabilities
Refreshments	Tea room open 11:00 am to 4:30 pm on same days as battery
Toilets	Within the battery
Dogs	Dogs and children must be kept under strict control because of the cliffs

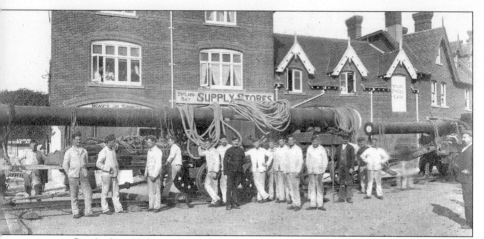

Barrels of two 9-2 in. gun barrels being hauled through Totland on their way to the New Needles in about 1914. The barrels, each one weighing about 28 tonnes, were landed at Colwell Bay and hauled up to the battery by horses using sections of railway track fitted to wooden sleepers. (Eric Toogood)

The Needles Old Battery was completed in 1863 as part of the concerted plan to defend the Solent area from French attack. Thirty years later the original guns were replaced by larger ordnance. However, when they began firing these, rockfalls began to occur on the cliff face. As a consequence, it was decided to build a new battery higher up the cliff. It was at this time that the road along the headland was constructed. Previously transport had been along a track across the top of the downs. From 1956 to 1971, the Needles headland was used by Saunders-Roe as a static test site for rocket engines. These engines were developed on the Island for use in the Black Knight and Black Arrow space rockets. The concrete base for the test site remains and there is an information board and photographs describing the project.

Within the Needles Pleasure Park is a memorial to Guglielmo Marconi, the "Father of Radio". His early work was rejected by the Italian Government. In 1896, after failing to get support for his project elsewhere, he ended up in England, developing his wireless equipment for the General Post Office. After proving it in London and Salisbury, he set up the world's first permanent wireless station at Alum Bay in 1897. Here he gradually extended the range of reception up to forty miles. In 1900, a wireless telegraphy station was established at Niton. This was later used to transmit Morse code messages to ships in the English

Channel. Using this research Marconi, eventually developed a system for transmitting the sound of the human voice. In February 1920, the first public broadcast was made using this system. In 1922, the BBC was formed and regular programmes began to be broadcast.

Alum Bay became a tourist attraction because of the multicoloured sands that form the cliffs. The sands were collected, dried and sold in glass phials or made into sand paintings. A pier was built in about 1873 to allow pleasure steamers to stop in the bay. This photograph shows the pier in about 1890, after its rebuilding in 1886-7, with the excursion steamers PS Leopold and PS Heather Belle alongside. The pier was severely damaged in a storm in 1929 and was never rebuilt. (George Hook)

Totland Bay Pier was built in 1880 and was used by pleasure steamers from Bournemeouth during the summer months. This photograph shows PS Solent approaching the pier in about 1920. (Allan Insole)

After visiting the sharp end of the Island, the itinerary now returns eastward. Return along Alum Bay New Road, staying on it until you come to the first road on your left, Headon Rise. This will take you to Cliff Road above Totland Bay, from where you can look down on Totland Pier. This was built in 1880 at the same time as the large Totland Bay Hotel to cater for the Victorian upper class holiday makers. As time passed and fashions changed, the hotel gradually lost favour and was eventually demolished. The village of Totland was carved out of the area called Freshwater in 1894. In the Broadway are the offices of The West Wight Beacon, Sherwood Stores and Post Office. These premises have copies of the Totland Village Trail in stock.

From the Broadway continue along Colwell Road until, on the right at the top of a hill, there is a sign indicating The Palmerston Inn and Golden Hill Fort. Turn right, off the road, past the works, watching out for the short steep humps as you go. Park in the car park on the right of the narrow passage leading through the embankment surrounding the fort.

3.8	Golden Hill Fort

A fortified garrison built in 1867 to serve the fortifications built against possible French invasion. Military museum containing a variety of artefacts of the Island military scene and WW2 with audio-visual presentation in the Garrison Cinema; period costumes and dresses. Also within the complex is the largest HO model railway in the country with a maximum run of 200 feet and up to 35 minutes between repeat movements using the latest state of the art computer control; complete with operational road vehicles and other features; suitable for adults and older children. There is also a collection of Messerschmitt bubble cars.

Location	Colwell Road/Norton Green Road junction
Operator	Lodge Pass Ltd.
Telephone no.	753380
Opening hours	10:00 am to 6:00 pm daily, Easter to end of October
Admission charges	£1.50; additional charge of £3.00 to enter model railway exhibition
Parking	By approach road to fort
Bus route	Southern Vectis nos. 7, 7A & 42

Disabled access	Wheelchair access to ground floor plus chair lift to first floor
Refreshments	Cafe/restaurant, ice cream parlour and bar in the fort
Toilets	In the fort
Dogs	Admitted on lead

Return to the main road and turn sharp right into Norton Green Road. At the end of this road turn right again into Copse Lane. At the T-junction with Hooke Hill, turn left. Park outside All Saint's Church where there is limited parking. In the church yard, turn left and follow the boundary wall to a small flint building. This houses an exhibition devoted the life and works of the scientist Hooke.

3.9	**Hookeiana, All Saint's Room Beyond Time**

Exhibition detailing the fascinating life of the talented 17th century scientist, Robert Hooke, who was born in Freshwater; the displays include examples of some of his work.

Location	The Bier House in the grounds of All Saint's Church, Freshwater
Operator	Mr. T. Clarke (Hooke Society)
Telephone no.	756614
Opening hours	10:00 am to 1:00 pm and 2:00 pm to 4:30 pm, Tuesdays and Thursdays
Admission charges	Free
Parking	Limited parking outside church (leave room for funeral parties); alternatively use public car park off School Green Road
Bus route	Southern Vectis nos. 7, 7A, 7B, 7C (at other end of Hooke Hill Road)
Disabled access	Wheelchair access
Refreshments	Red Lion Inn, Church Place
Toilets	In museum
Dogs	No dogs

Near the roundabout at the eastern end of School Green Road is a monument to Hooke. Near the same roundabout is a foodstore owned by the Portsea Island Mutual Co-operative Society. This stands on the site of the Acorn Spring Works. This replaced the Freshwater terminal of the Freshwater, Yarmouth & Newport Railway after the closing of the line by British Railways in 1953.

Isle of Wight Central Railway 2-4-0 tank Osborne at Freshwater station shortly after its opening in 1889. (Eric Toogood)

Leave Church Place via the lane opposite the Red Lion Inn and cross the Causeway over the River Yar. Note the Second World War pill box machine-gun post on the right at the start of the Causeway. Beyond the Causeway, the road crosses the track of the old Freshwater, Yarmouth & Newport Railway. The house on the left was the crossing keeper's cottage. Immediately after this, on the right, is the drive to Afton Manor, a private house which is hidden by a fairly dense copse. The present building dates from the early 18th century but the manor itself dates back to before the Norman Conquest.

At the end of the Causeway, turn left onto the B3401 Newport Road and continue for about four and a half miles. At a sharp rise and right-hand bend in the road is Calbourne Mill. It is difficult to miss it since there is a 38 ton cannon beside the road. This was one of a battery of four such guns in Cliff End Battery, near Colwell Bay. The gun is 19 feet 2 inches long with a 12 1/2 inch rifled bore.

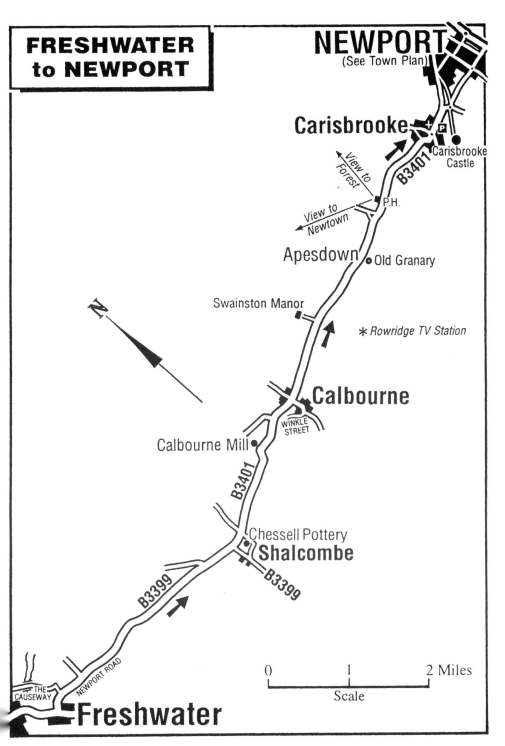

FRESHWATER to NEWPORT

NEWPORT
(See Town Plan)

Carisbrooke

Carisbrooke Castle

B3401

P.H.

View to Forest

View to Newtown

Apesdown

Old Granary

Swainston Manor

*Rowridge TV Station

N

Calbourne

WINKLE STREET

Calbourne Mill

B3401

Chessell Pottery

Shalcombe

B3399

B3399

NEWPORT ROAD

THE CAUSEWAY

Freshwater

0   1   2 Miles
Scale

3.10 Calbourne Water Mill & Museum of Rural Life

The mill was listed in the Domesday Book and continued to work as a flour mill until 1955; it is now preserved and demonstrates how a watermill worked; collection of agricultural implements, domestic antiques and a fire engine.

Location	Freshwater Hill, Calbourne
Operator	Geo. Weeks & Son Ltd.
Telephone no.	531227
Opening hours	10:00 am to 6:00 pm, daily, Easter to end of October
Admission charges	Adults £2.50, children £1.00, senior citizens £1.50
Parking	Car park next to mill
Bus route	Southern Vectis no. 7C
Disabled access	Wheelchair access to ground floor only
Refreshments	Tea room
Toilets	On site
Dogs	On a lead

From Calbourne Mill, continue on the B3401 for about half a mile to the Sun Inn. Turn right into Calbourne village. The lane is narrow and parking can be difficult here, the best place being by the church. The second turning on the right is Barrington Row, commonly known as Winkle Street. This is an unspoilt row of elderly country cottages with a stream running down opposite the side of the lane. Half way along the stream is an ancient sheepwash. At one time there were many sheep in the Calbourne area and one of the common rights was the use of the sheepwash. Traditionally, sheep were sent through a wash to clean the wool a few days before shearing began. Walk to the end of Winkle Street and continue down the path beyond, CB15. This leads to the site of another, less well known, mill in Calbourne. In the 14th century, there was a fulling mill next to the road. At that time there were six such mills on the Island for fulling woven cloth, that is pounding it into a thicker, compressed mass, thus making it stronger and smoother.

Return to the cross roads and turn right. A mile further along the main road, Swainston Manor can be seen on the left. There is a record of a grant of land here to the Monastery of St. Swithuns in Winchester in the year 735. In 827, the same monastery received the rest of the manor of Calbourne from King Egbert. The Abbot of the Monastery of St. Swithuns was the Bishop of Winchester and, for several centuries, Swainston was his summer palace. The house is now an hotel and popular restaurant. The oldest visible part of the building is the stone-built chapel and hall, believed to date from the 12th century, with its external wooden staircase.

From Swainston, the road to Newport gradually rises. There is then a long straight descent through overhanging trees. Near the bottom of this descent is a place strangely called Apesdown and, on the right-hand side of the road, are some farm buildings with a good example of a granary standing on staddle stones. The staddle stones lift the granary off the ground and prevent rats gaining access to the stored grain.

Nearer Newport, the car park of the Blacksmiths Arms provides an excellent view of the ancient harbour of Newtown. In medieval times, Newtown became a Freetown by grant of charter and sent two members to Parliament until 1832, as did Yarmouth and Newport. Also to the left, but closer to the viewpoint, is Great Park Farm. This name records the presence here in early medieval times of the "King's park", an area of forest surrounded by a bank and fence to protect breeding deer. The offspring were used to replenish the stock in the unenclosed royal hunting forest which surrounded it and whose remnant, Parkhurst Forest, can be seen to the right.

There follow more views over the Medina valley as the narrow road approaches Newport. The road then drops steeply to the top of Carisbrooke High Street. Continue across the roundabout, down past the church to the public car park on your right. From here walk back up the hill to visit the Norman Priory Church of St. Mary's. Opposite St. Mary's, a narrow lane, Castle Street, leads down to a ford across Lukely Brook. This apparently insignificant stream was a major source of power before the introduction of steam. Carisbrooke Mill, which lies just upstream of the ford, was one of seven water mills between Carisbrooke and Newport Quay powered by Lukely Brook. Return to the main road and walk down to the Eight Bells Inn where, at the back, is the mill pond which powered the second mill.

Drive on into Newport and take the first road, Recreation Ground Road, on the left after the garage. This road crosses the Lukely Brook. Stop beside the stream and look through the trees on the left for a glimpse of another mill house. Turn right before the Victoria Recreation Ground gates (1896) and along Wilver Road until it bends right to cross the brook again. Do not cross this bridge but fork left into Westminster Lane, which runs alongside the stream. The road narrows as it turns past Westminster Mill, which has been converted into flats. Continue past the dairy, built on the site of yet another mill powered by Lukely Brook. Turn right and then left into Crocker Street. On the right, about half way down this street, is a large public car park.

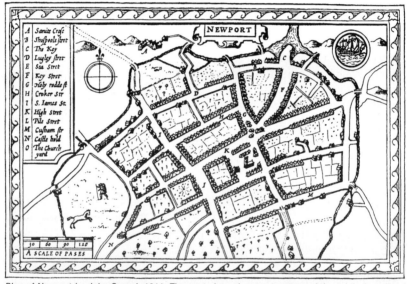

Plan of Newport by John Speed, 1611. The central regular street pattern of the original medieval town is still apparent. However, at this time, Newport was in the middle of a period of prosperity. Open sites along the original streets were being infilled and the town was beginning to encroach on the surrounding open land. (Peter Gustar)

From the Crocker Street car park, it is a short walk back past the telephone exchange to the small house on the left whose owners have restored the original name board over the window indicating that it was once a saddlery. Walking back past the car park, the Worsley Almshouses, founded in 1618, are on the right. These have recently been restored and were awarded a plaque by the Isle of Wight Society for the excellence of the result. Cross Lower St. James' Street and walk along the continuation of Crocker Street beyond. On your left, at the first floor level at number 62 is a reproduction of a wooden figure mounted in a niche. This building was a school for poor girls who received a basic education and were taught how to carry out domestic work so that they could find employment as servants. The school began in Lugley Street in 1761 but moved here in 1880. The girls wore a distinctive uniform and hence the wooden figure became known as "The Blue Jenny". Further along the street, on the left, look out for the metal grills over the windows of the old Mew's Brewery buildings and the conical top of the malting house. These buildings were converted into sheltered accommodation and are an excellent example of how redundant industrial buildings can be adapted to suit modern needs.

The original Newport Blue School at 10 Lugley Street. In the niche above the entrance is the "The Blue Jenny", a wooden figurine painted in the blue uniform of the school. The school later moved to 62 Crocker Street, where it stayed until it was closed in 1907. The original carving is now in Carisbrooke Castle Museum, but a replica figure was placed in the niche at the Crocker Street premises in 1980 thanks to the efforts of the Newport Group of the Isle of Wight Society. (Roy Brinton)

At the end of Crocker Street turn right and then right again at the next junction into Lugley Street. Walk along this street to the next cross-roads. On the right-hand corner opposite, is a stone building which used to house the old Newport Grammar School. This was founded by a group of local gentlemen and the school building was constructed between 1614 and 1619. For over two months in the autumn of 1648, the building was used for the negotiations between King Charles I and the Parliamentary Commissioners on the abortive Treaty of Newport. During this period, it is believed that the king stayed at a house on the corner of Holyrood Street and Lugley Street. Continue along Lugley Street to return to the Crocker Street car park.

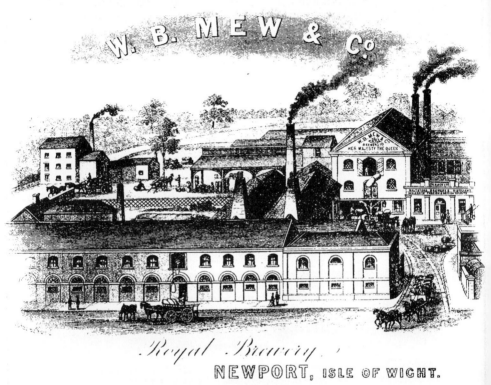

Lithograph of W.B. Mew & Co. Royal Brewery, about 1870. (Allan Insole)

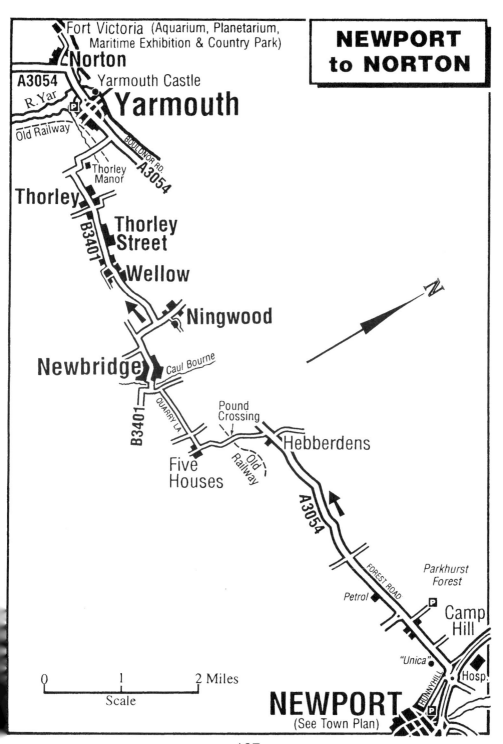

NEWPORT to NORTON

Fort Victoria (Aquarium, Planetarium, Maritime Exhibition & Country Park)

Norton

A3054

R.Yar

Yarmouth Castle

Yarmouth

Old Railway

BOULDNOR RD.

A3054

Thorley Manor

Thorley

Thorley Street

B3401

Wellow

Ningwood

Newbridge

Caul Bourne

QUARRY LA.

B3401

Pound Crossing

Old Railway

Five Houses

Hebberdens

A3054

Forest Road

Parkhurst Forest

Petrol

Camp Hill

"Unica"

Hosp.

HOUNNXHILL

NEWPORT

(See Town Plan)

0   1   2 Miles

Scale

4. THE NORTH-WEST FACET

Newport — Newbridge — Wellow — Thorley — Norton — Yarmouth — Shalfleet — Porchfield — Cowes — Northwood — Parkhurst

This itinerary starts in the car park beside Lukely Brook at the bottom of Hunny Hill. This is the site of the demolished Town Gate Mill. Walk across the Town Gate Bridge over the brook and turn right into the small private car park. The green corrugated iron building at the entrance to the car park, opposite the Red Cross Headquarters, was originally the main offices of the Freshwater, Yarmouth and Newport Railway Company! At the far end of the car park is a notice board which provides information about the St. Cross Priory, built in 1120, which originally stood here and the St. Cross Mill which subsequently occupied the site.

Towngate Mill, Newport, was built on the Lukely Brook alongside Hunnyhill Bridge in the early 19th century. The millwheel was sited beneath the trees at the right-hand end of the building. This photograph appears to have been taken in about 1875. (Allan Insole)

There is also an explanation of the remains of a railway viaduct which stands adjacent to the mill. This carried the Freshwater, Yarmouth & Newport Railway line across the valley and was built in the late 1880's. The path next to the viaduct climbs up to the modern Newport bypass., built on the site of Newport Railway Station. The bridge that carries the road over the harbour replaced one that carried the railway lines heading to east Wight.

Return to the Hunny Hill car park. From the car park, drive up to the top of Hunny Hill. There is a rather complex junction here by a large roundabout. The road you require is the A3054 to Yarmouth which involves a right, followed immediately, by a left turn into Forest Road. About a hundred yards along this road, on the left, is a round prefabricated house called Unica. This is a structure was designed by Sam Saunders, an East Cowes boat and plane builder. It was originally erected in the late 1920's but was later moved here. Its most unusual feature was that it was designed to be rotated in its entirety as required.

Forest Road runs alongside Parkhurst Forest, the remnant of a royal forest which originally stretched from the Medina valley west to Newtown. It would not have been a "forest" in the modern sense but a mix of woodland and heathland much like the New Forest is today. It is now sadly reduced to a thousand acres of mixed woodland. During the Napoleonic Wars, many oaks were felled here for shipbuilding at Cowes. Three quarters of a mile along the road, just after a wooden building on the right, is an entrance to the forest. A quarter of a mile along the track is a car park with an information board. There are several trails through the forest which start from this car park.

Three and a half miles beyond the edge of Parkhurst Forest, take a left hand fork down Pounds Lane and signposted to Five Houses. Half a mile along this lane is Pound Crossing which used to be a level crossing over the Newport to Freshwater railway line, which closed in 1953. At Fivehouses, turn to the right and at the next cross-roads, go straight ahead along Quarry Lane towards Newbridge. The road name of the road records that there was once a quarry here, one of a number in this area which supplied limestone for building. Quarry Lane joins the Newbridge Road just before the bridge crossing the Caul Bourne. Turn right and climb up the hill into the village of Newbridge - it was called Newbryge 600 years ago! At Malthouse Green (and shop), at the top of the hill, a car may be parked.

Pound Crossing, near Five Houses with the gate keepers, Mr. and Mrs. Rickman. (Eric Toogood)

Walk back down the hill to the bridge and take the path, S35, to the north alongside the stream. This stream feeds the Calbourne Lower Mill pond. About three hundred yards along the footpath, it is possible to cross the stream to the mill. The mill worked until 1976 and the bread ovens were used commercially for some time afterwards. This mill is somewhat unusual because the millpond feeds into the mill at first floor level. This can clearly be seen from the lane leading south from the mill. Continue down the lane to the Newbridge Road and follow it up into the village.

From Newbridge, continue west on the B3401 through the small hamlets of Wellow and Thorley Street. At the T-junction just beyond the latter, turn right towards Yarmouth. Directly ahead is Thorley Manor. The sheltered Thorley Creek, beyond the house, was a harbour long before Yarmouth was founded. In pre-Norman times, this was one of the main crossing points to the mainland and an important manor. However, silting up of the shallow creek eventually made it useable only at high tide. A new landing place was therefore made at the mouth of the Yar and from this developed the town of Yarmouth. In the Domesday Survey of 1086, Thorley was valued at £12 compared with Yarmouth's value of 25 shillings, but within 50 years the position had been completely reversed.

The present Thorley Manor was built in 1712 and is the fifth house known to have been built on the site. It was a new design for the Island, showing a swing away from the E-shape groundplan typical of the 17th century manor houses towards a more classical design. Just beyond the manor house is a small mortuary chapel based on the restored remains of a 13th century belfry. Over the years, the settlement had gradually moved up the hill away from the manor house and creek. In 1871, the old church was dismantled and a new one built in the centre of the village. The belfry was left behind in the move.

From Thorley Manor, continue along Thorley Road. This follows the line of the old medieval track which twisted from shingle bank to shingle bank across the creek. In winter this area still floods. A short circular walk begins in the car park on the right, just after the bridge over Thorley Brook. The footpath follows the old railway track to Yarmouth station. By the mid-18th century, Thorley Creek had silted up and an embankment was built across it. This created a tidal pond for a tide mill which was built in 1793 at the mouth of the creek. As the tide rose, the sea was allowed to flow into the tide pond. At high tide, the sluices were closed. As the tide ebbed, water flowed from the pond through the mill driving the mill wheel and machinery in the northern part of the building. The southern end was the millers house. The system imposed a shift system on the workers since they had to work according to the tides. The mill was very efficient and grain was even brought here from the mainland to be milled. In 1888, the railway embankment taking the line from Yarmouth to Freshwater was built across the tidemill pond. This reduced the volume of water available to drive the mill wheel. To get around this problem a steam pump was introduced. The stump of the chimney of the boiler house can be seen at the northern end of the building. However, this new technology failed to save the mill and it ceased operating. A path leads back along the south side of Thorley Brook to the car park.

At the T-junction with Bouldnor Road, turn left towards Yarmouth. Pass around the edge of Yarmouth and over the new bridge over the western River Yar. This bridge, built in 1987, replaced the one built in 1863. Until that time, the only access to the land west of the river was a ferry across the creek here or, for vehicles, via the beach at Freshwater Bay.

On the other side of the Yar Valley, the road bends sharply left. Two hundred yards farther on, take the road on the right, signposted to Fort Victoria Country Park. The lane crests the brow of a low hill and descends sharply towards the Solent, before turning left parallel to the beach. At the end is a car park on the site of the barracks for Fort Victoria.

The remains here are those of a brick-built fort constructed in 1852 as a defence against the French. There were placements for heavy guns at sea-level in the large triangular fortification which still exists plus somewhat lighter guns on the first floor and roof of the now demolished barracks. As is often the case with military technology, the fort was out-of-date almost before it was completed. It was consequently given over to the Royal Engineers, who used it as a base for their mine laying and searchlight experiments in the 1890's. The pier immediately to the east was extended to give 18 feet of water at low tide and stores were landed here for the all the fortifications and barracks in the area during both World Wars. Recent attempts to demolish the pier failed completely! In 1962, the fort was abandoned by the Army and in 1969 it was almost completely demolished. What remains houses a fascinating collection. Starting on the left is an information board about the country park, toilets, the Park Ranger's base, a café and then three exhibitions.

Fort Victoria pier was developed in the 1860's from an old wooden Coastguard landing stage. It was used to offload troops and supplies for Fort Victoria and other forts in the area. This photograph shows a group of Territorial coast gunners landing in 1916. These troops attended annual camps at Cliff End Battery. (George Hook)

4.1   Marine Heritage Exhibition

A display in three sections. The first part exhibition deals with underwater archaeology and shipwrecks, using three dimensional scenes and recovered objects to open a window onto the seabed, marine excavations and life on board a 16th century ship. The second area deals with the prehistoric Solent at the end of the last Ice Age when the area was dry land; an audio-visual display takes you back in time to learn of the animals and men who occupied in the Solent river valley at that time. The final section tells the story of the fort and its role in defending the entrance to the Solent. Shop selling books etc.

Location   Fort Victoria, Westhill Road, Norton, near Yarmouth
Operator   The Hampshire and Isle of Wight Trust for Maritime Archaeology
Telephone no.   761214
Opening hours   10:00 am to 5:00 pm daily, Easter to end of September
Admission charges Adults 75p, children and senior citizens 40p
Parking   Public car park
Bus route   Southern Vectis no.7, 7A & 42
Disabled access   Wheelchair access
Refreshments   Cafe
Toilets   On site
Dogs   On a lead

4.2   Fort Victoria Planetarium

A visit to the planetarium is an adventure, a voyage into space to learn about our place in the Universe, astronomy and space exploration. Books and videos on sale.

Location   Fort Victoria, Westhill Road, Norton, near Yarmouth
Operator   Mr. P. England
Telephone no.   761555

Opening hours	10:00 am to 5:30 pm daily from Easter to October; afternoons only on winter Saturdays and Sundays; special evening shows can be arranged
Admission charges	Adults £2.00, children £1.40, family and senior citizen reductions
Parking	Public car park
Bus route	Southern Vectis nos. 7, 7A & 42
Disabled access	Wheelchair access
Refreshments	Cafe
Toilets	On site
Dogs	On a lead

4.3 Fort Victoria Marine Aquarium

An introduction to the fish and invertebrates, from flatfish to conger eels, starfish to cuttlefish, which can live in the sea around the Island and have been inhabiting these waters for thousands of years.

Location	Fort Victoria, Westhill Road, Norton, near Yarmouth
Operator	Mr. N. Blake
Telephone no.	760283
Opening hours	10:00 am to 6:00 pm daily from Easter to October
Admission charges	Adults £1.50, children and senior citizens 75p
Parking	Public car park
Bus route	Southern Vectis nos. 7, 7A & 42
Disabled access	Wheelchairs access
Refreshments	Cafe
Toilets	On site
Dogs	On a lead

From the south-western side of Fort Victoria Country Park, you can see Fort Albert. This was built in 1856 but, like Fort Victoria, soon became obsolete. In 1887, it was modified for experiments on a new secret weapon, the Brennan Locomotive Torpedo, the first wire guided torpedo. A launching ramp was built on the north side, with a torpedo store and wire winding shed behind it. The northern two thirds of the fort were filled with sea sand to protect the torpedo installation against explosions. The torpedo station ceased operations in 1906 and was finally abandoned in 1956. The fort has recently been converted into luxury flats.

A short walk east of the Fort Victoria car park, there are a pair of large metal "stanchions" at the top of the beach. These were used during the recovery of the cruiser *HMS Gladiator*, which sank off Fort Victoria after a colliding with the American liner *St. Paul* during a freak snowstorm in April, 1908. 27 members of the *Gladiator*'s crew were drowned in the accident but the remainder of the complement of 260 men were rescued thanks to the bravery of the Royal Engineers stationed in the fort. The *Gladiator* was salvaged, repaired and then almost immediately scrapped!

HMS Gladiator *being salvaged in September, 1908, an activity which attracted a large number of spectators. (Sylvia Taylor)*

Retrace the route back to Yarmouth. As the Yar bridge is approached, a stone-built building, usually surrounded by yachts, can be seen on the left. This is known as the Sand House. In the late 18th century, it was used to store sand carted overland from Alum Bay before it was exported to the mainland. The sand was used in the potteries in Staffordshire and Worcester and for glass making in Bristol. Adjacent to the Sand House may be seen remnants of the older bridge. Cross the new bridge and follow the main road round to the right where there is a large public car park on reclaimed land. This car park makes a suitable starting point for a circular walking tour of the town.

The Sand House was used to store sand brought overland from Alum Bay until about 1850. The building later became a coal store and today it forms part of Hayles Boatyard. (Eric Toogood)

Yarmouth has a long and prestigious history having been granted more Royal Charters, five dating between 1135 and 1560, than any other town in England. From the car-park, walk north alongside the quay. The Tourist Information Office is in Quay Street, opposite the ferry marshalling area. A copy of a Yarmouth Trail can be purchased here. Adjacent to the ferry terminal is Yarmouth Castle. The entrance is down a short alley.

Yarmouth Castle was completed in 1547, one of Henry VIII's chain of coastal defences. It represented the latest thinking in military engineering. Unlike Henry's earlier forts, most of which were round, Yarmouth is square with a fine example of an arrow shaped bastion at one corner. While washed by the Solent on two sides, the other two were defended by a moat. Yarmouth was an important Parliamentary stronghold during the Civil War. It was garrisoned well into the 19th century.

4.4 Yarmouth Castle

An unspoilt Henry VIII castle with commanding view of the western Solent; exhibition of paintings of the Isle of Wight, photographs of Yarmouth and the development of fortifications. Shop with informative books, souvenirs, etc.

Location	Quay Street
Operator	English Heritage
Telephone no.	760678
Opening hours	10:00 am to 6:00 pm daily from 1st April to 30th Sept
Admission charges	Adults £1.70, children 85p, senior citizens £1.25; free to English Heritage members
Parking	Public car park 300yds
Bus route	Southern Vectis nos. 7, 7A & 42
Disabled access	Wheelchair access to ground floor only
Refreshments	Several cafes and restaurants in vicinity
Toilets	Between the castle and ferry terminal
Dogs	Admitted on a lead

Yarmouth harbour and the Town Quay about 1900. Yarmouth originally had an open harbour but a breakwater was built in 1843-47 on the Norton side to form an enclosed area. In 1858 an embankment and a bridge were built across the southern end of the harbour. The harbour was dredged in 1938 and the original quay has been extended to form the ferry terminal. In the distance is the wooden pier built in 1876. (Allan Insole)

From the castle, walk along Quay Street, past the George Hotel and into The Square. Turn left and walk along Pier Street to the entrance to Yarmouth Pier. The pier is 700 feet long and was completed in 1876 at a cost of £4,000. Although there was a shallow water quay in the harbour, the paddle steamers trading along the south coast required deeper water. The loan took 50 years to pay off! The pier is constructed of wood and is constantly under attack from the elements. From the pier, walk south through The Square. On your right is the Town Hall, with an inscription recording the rebuilding of 1763. Further south is the Parish Church of 1614. Turn right at the next road junction and walk back a short distance to the car park.

From Yarmouth, proceed east along the Bouldnor Road towards Newport. A small lay-by at the end of Bouldnor Road provides a view over the western Solent. After a mile the main A3054 road passes a straggle of ribbon development on the left, part of the scattered community of Cranmore. Take the next turning on the right, signposted to Wellow and Newbridge and opposite the Horse & Groom Inn. This road is Station Road and used to lead to Ningwood Railway Station. A few hundred yards along this road, on the left, is Ningwood Manor. This manor is mentioned in the Domesday Book. The rear of the present building is of 17th century origin while the Georgian front was added by John Pinhorn in 1784.

Beyond Ningwood Manor House, turn left into the narrow Warlands Lane which wanders across country until you reach the main Yarmouth-Newport road again. Turn right into the village of Shalfleet, whose name is derived from the Saxon for "a shallow creek". Parking in the main road is difficult but there is a small car park along Mill Lane. To reach this, turn sharp left at the traffic lights. Shalfleet parish church, St. Michael's, is well worth a visit. It is a very massive structure built in Norman times and there is a magnificent Romanesque carved tympanum over the north door. The tower is strongly fortified with walls five feet thick and no external door. It once housed the town gun for defence against the French. In 1377 and again in 1524, when Yarmouth was sacked by the French, the people of Shalfleet found protection in their church.

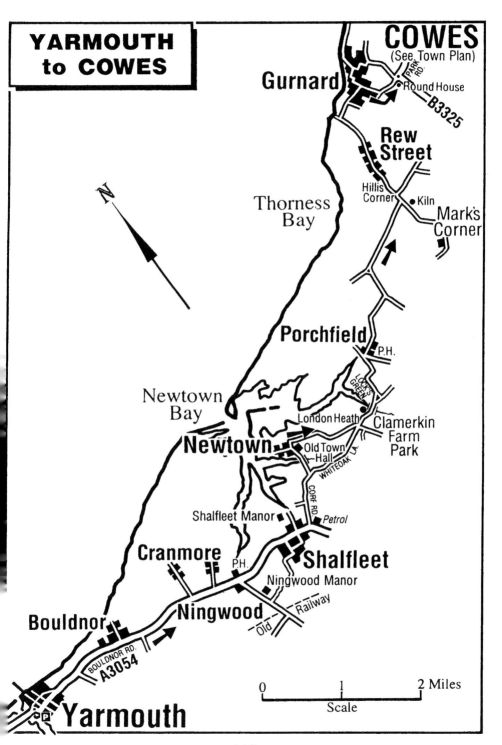

YARMOUTH to COWES

COWES (See Town Plan)

Gurnard
Round House
B3325

Rew Street

Hillis Corner
Kiln
Mark's Corner

Thorness Bay

Porchfield
P.H.

LOCK'S GREEN

Newtown Bay

London Heath
Clamerkin Farm Park

Newtown
Old Town Hall
WHITEOAK LA.

CORF RD.

Shalfleet Manor
Petrol

Cranmore
P.H.
Shalfleet

Ningwood Manor

Bouldnor
Ningwood
Old Railway

BOULDNOR RD.
A3054

Yarmouth

0   1   2 Miles
Scale

119

Opposite the church is Shalfleet Manor house, hidden behind dense foliage. The manor dates back to Domesday times when it was valued at fifteen pounds. The present house was built about 1630. Part of the rear of the Manor House can be seen from Mill Lane as you return to the car park. The house on the right at the end of Mill Lane is Shalfleet Mill, the last mill powered by the Caul Bourne on its way to the Solent. The peak of trade for mills on the Island was in the early 19th century when a combination of an increasing local population and the arrival of large military garrisons produced a heavy demand for flour. A decline in milling set in after 1850 when the garrisons began to be reduced. By the end of the century, many of the water wheels had been replaced by more efficient water turbines.

At the end of Mill Lane, a track through a gate to the left leads past the head of the creek to a stone quay. This is Shalfleet Quay and was once a busy commercial harbour where, amongst other things, coal was imported to the Island. Today it is busy at summer weekends with yachtsmen rushing ashore after their long passage across the Solent, following in ancient footsteps to refresh themselves at the New Inn.

On the main road a quarter of a mile east of Shalfleet, turn left into Corf Road. Half a mile down this road, take the second on the left signposted to Newtown. After crossing an old bridge, at the top of a hill, is the 18th century Newtown Town Hall, now standing in splendid isolation. Park in the car park just beyond the building.

4.5   Newtown Old Town Hall

Plain and simple chambers of the town hall with the town crest and a few artefacts; good information boards outside. In the chamber here just twelve Burgesses elected two Members of Parliament, generally over an oyster lunch! This "rotten borough" was abolished by the 1832 Reform Act, which resulted in the whole Island having just two M.P.'s!

Location	Town Lane, Newtown
Operator	The National Trust
Telephone no.	741052
Opening hours	2:00 pm to 4:45 pm, Sunday to Thursday in July and August; Monday, Wednesday and Sunday only from 30th March to 30th June and from 1st Sept to 30th October; also open Good Friday and Easter Saturday

Admission charges	£1.10; children 60p, free to National Trust members
Parking	N.T. car park on left just past building
Bus route	Southern Vectis no. 35
Disabled access	No access for wheelchairs
Refreshments	None
Toilets	None
Dogs	Dogs on a lead

Newtown was once one of the most important towns of the Island due mainly to its large sheltered harbour, which could accommodate ships of all sizes. The Bishop of Winchester founded the town in 1218 with the name Francheville and it was granted a Charter to hold a market. The town was laid out on a grid pattern leading down to the quay on the western side. This pattern can still be traced today, although some of the roads are traceable only as footpaths. In 1377 the town was sacked by the French and it never recovered its status.

Aerial view of Newtown and the estuary of the Newtown River in 1971 showing part of the grid pattern of the town. In the middle distance are salterns and the quay with a derelict salt boiling shed beside it. (Roger Smith)

From the town hall, walk down the road into the remains of the town. On the right, just beyond the town hall, is the former Noah's Ark public house, which bears the old Francheville Arms on its wall. It is now owned by the National Trust. Beyond Noah's Ark, one of the old road runs off left past the church. This eventually leads to a path down to Newtown Creek. To the left of the causeway here are the old saltpans where sea water was collected and evaporated in rectangular ponds during the summer months. The resulting brine was boiled in vats. The crumbling brick building with corrugated iron roof is the last remaining boiling house. The salt was very important, because, along with smoking, it was the only means of preserving meat before the advent of the tin and refrigerator.

The tidal area on the right of the causeway, partly enclosed by a sea wall, was at one time reclaimed for pasture. The storms of 1952 breached the wall and destroyed years of hard work overnight. It is now a tidal saltmarsh and forms a vital part of Newtown Nature Reserve. The creek to the east, called Clamerkin Lake, has extensive oyster beds, once a common feature of many of the creeks around the Solent.

Drive out of Newtown along Town Lane, past Old Vicarage Lane (where the Newtown Vicarage is a National Trust property), until the road junction at London Heath is reached. Turn left along White Oak Lane for about three hundred yards to Clamerkin Farm.

4.6   Clamerkin Farm Park

Woodland farmstead based around a reconstruction of a semi-permanent settlement of about 1000 A.D. with thatch and wattle dwellings; presentation of woodland crafts. Island brickmaking exhibition. This is also a place for youngsters to see and become friendly with domestic farm animals.

Location	White Oak Road, London Heath, near Porchfield
Operator	Mr. P. Hindle
Telephone no.	531396
Opening hours	10:30 am to 6:00 pm, daily, Easter to end of October
Admission charges	Adults £1.60, children 60p, senior citizens £1.20
Parking	In the grounds
Bus route	Southern Vectis no. 35

Disabled access	Access for wheelchairs
Refreshments	Cafe and picnic area
Toilets	On site
Dogs	On a lead

From Clamerkin Farm Park, proceed eastwards over Clamerkin Bridge towards Porchfield, keeping left at the next junction. At Locks Green, a large building is passed which looks like a manor house. It was, in fact, built as the local school in 1867, but closed many years ago as the local farming population declined. Continue on through Porchfield, passing the Sportsman's Rest, along the road towards Cowes. At Hillis Corner, turn right into Hillis Lane. About 150 yards down the road, standing in a private garden on the left-hand side of the road, is the last remaining "beehive" brick kiln on the Island. Return back to Hillis Corner and the main road. Turn right and at the mini roundabout, head left towards Gurnard. This lane is Rew Street, on which are some ancient farm buildings, including a classic four-bay cart shed on the left, now sadly altered. At the foot of the hill is the coast and Gurnard Luck - "luck" being an Island word for an inlet or pond fed by the sea. This has been used as a landing place for centuries. The Romans built a villa here on the coast but it was eroded away by the sea in the 19th century.

A four-bay cart shed with a timber-framed front at Baskett's Farm, Rew Street photographed in 1978. It has since been converted into a house. (Allan Insole)

The road now runs along the shingle bank separating Gurnard Marshes from the sea. At the end of the marshes, it climbs a hill into the modern suburbia of Gurnard. At the top of the hill, turn right into Worsley Road. Follow the road out of Gurnard, across a small valley and into the outskirts of Cowes. At the next junction is a roundabout, adjacent to which is a small completely round house built in the cottage orneé style. Opposite is one of the gatehouses designed by Nash for the Ward Estate. Carry on across the roundabout and start the long descent down Park Road towards the sea front. At the point when the Solent comes into view, turn right just before the tall block of flats into Granville Road. Take the first turn left onto Granville Bridge. This short road has an awkward shape because it used to be a bridge over the Cowes to Newport railway line. Park in the public car park here.

From the car park, walk down the hill into the shopping precinct. The supermarket just below the car park was built on the site of the old Cowes Railway Station. At the bottom of the hill, turn right. Walk to the end of the pedestrianised shopping area. There are some interesting old shop fronts in this part of Cowes, including a rare Art Nouveau frontage. At the end of the pedestrianised area, turn right into Beckford Road. A short distance up this road is the public library, within which is Cowes Maritime Museum.

4.7 Cowes Maritime Museum

Exhibition of models, paintings and photographs illustrating the former ship building industry of Cowes and East Cowes, which provided ships for the Navy over several centuries; collection of small boats from the modern yacht-building industry.

Location	The Library, Beckford Road
Operator	IW Council
Telephone no.	293341
Opening hours	9:30 am to 6:00 pm Monday to Wednesday and Friday; 9:30 am to 4:30 pm Saturday
Admission charges	Free
Parking	Public car parks in town
Bus route	Southern Vectis nos. 1, 1A, 2, 3, 30 & 91
Disabled access	Wheelchair access to ground floor only
Refreshments	Several cafes and restaurants in town
Toilets	In town
Dogs	On a lead

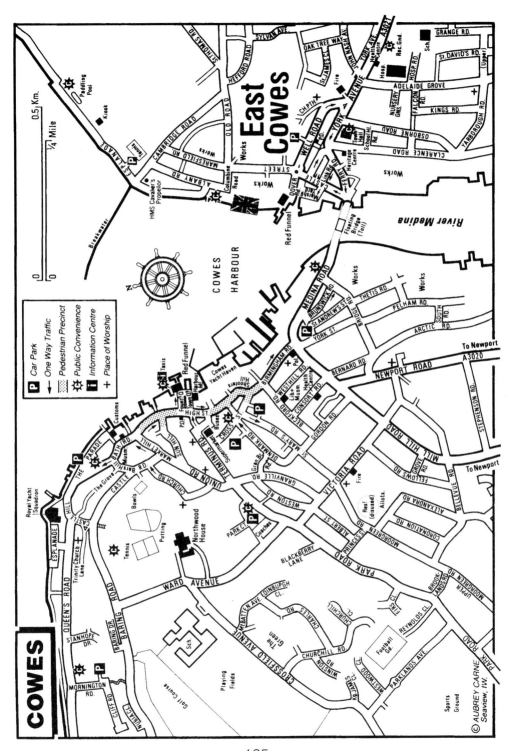

In the library you can purchase various publications on local features, including the Cowes Town Trail. Across the road from the library is the Cowes Voluntary Activity Centre. If you are in the vicinity on a Monday morning, the Local History Group meets here between 10:00 am and midday.

From Beckford Road walk back down the hill, through the shopping precinct and past the ferry terminal. A few yards past this, on the right, is The Prospect in which houses the Sir Max Aitken Museum.

4.8	Sir Max Aitken Museum

There are regular guided tours of the museum which is housed in the old Ratsey's sail loft on the waterfront; museum contains the many and varied treasures collected by Sir Max during his busy life; many items have connections with his special interest in sailing and while others have royal connections (such as Queen Victoria's croquet set).

Location	The Prospect, High Street
Operator	Max Aitken Museum Trust
Telephone no.	295144
Opening hours	10:00 am to 4:00 pm, daily, May to end of September
Admission charges	Adults £1.00, children and senior citizens 50p
Parking	Car parks in the town
Bus route	Southern Vectis nos. 1, 1A, 2, 3, 30 & 91
Disabled access	No access for wheelchairs
Refreshments	Several cafes and restaurants nearby
Toilets	In the town
Dogs	No dogs

From The Prospect continue along the High Street until a twitten or narrow alley appears on the right. This is Watch House Lane, named after the Customs House, and leads down to the Esplanade. A small pier was built here in 1901 and was used by paddle steamers taking day trips to and from the Island. It was demolished after the end of the Second World War.

Victoria Pier, Cowes, about 1910. It was built in 1901 by the local council to be used by the many pleasure steamers that plied the Solent throughout the summer season. The pier was found to be unsafe and was demolished in 1961. (Allan Insole)

At the far end of the Esplanade is Cowes Castle, built on the orders of Henry VIII to protect the harbour. It is now home of the world famous Royal Yacht Squadron. This was founded in 1815 to provide additional vessels for the nation's defence in time of need. The wealthy owners started racing their craft in 1826 when peace with France was established. The Squadron's original home was at the Medina Hotel in East Cowes. In 1856, Cowes Castle was leased from the Government and the freehold purchased in 1917. The 21 small brass cannons standing on the bastion in front of the Castle came from William IV's "yacht" *Royal Adelaide*. They are used to start and finish sailing races.

Beyond the Castle is Prince's Green, given to the town by George Stephenson, the railway engineer and son of the famous Robert Stephenson, builder of *The Rocket*. George Stephenson lived in a Victorian mansion beside the Green. From the Squadron, walk up Castle Hill. At the top of the hill, immediately opposite you are some steps which lead into the grounds of Northwood House. This is an imposing Grecian style mansion rebuilt in 1837 to a John Nash design for the Ward family. It is now local authority offices and chambers.

The Ward Estate was surrounded by a wall built in 1841. One of the conditions of the eventual sale of the property was that the walls should be maintained intact apart from the need for access. The walled estate stretched from the Castle Hill steps all the way to the Round House gatehouse passed on entering Cowes. Along all the boundary, sections of the wall can still be found.

Next to Northwood House is the church of St. Mary. The tower was built in 1815 and is another example of a Nash design. From Northwood House walk along Ward Avenue to Park Avenue and back to the car park near the centre of the town.

The next stage of the itinerary is complicated by the local one-way street system. Drive out of the car park and follow the one-way street system up St Mary's Road. Take the first turning on the left and then the first on the left again into Beckford Road. At the end of Beckford Road, turn left into Birmingham Road. Opposite the police station at the end of Birmingham Road is the house where Thomas Arnold, the son of a local Customs Officer, was born. The house bears an elaborate, locally manufactured brick plaque recording the fact. Thomas Arnold later became famous as the headmaster of Rugby School.

Turn left down Medina Road. On the left, behind a modern ship chandlers is a large concrete apron. On this site Saunders Roe manufactured seaplanes from 1916 until the blitz of 1942. In the 1960's the concrete apron was used as a hovercraft terminal. The hovercraft passenger service to Southampton regularly punctuated the sounds of the town with the loud roar of its propellers.

At the end of Medina Road is the Cowes terminus of the East Cowes-West Cowes chain ferry. On the far bank, to the right of the ferry terminal, there used to be tall cranes, large sheets of steel and the continuous racket of riveting as the workers of J.S. White's built their ships. The main offices of this company were in the stone building on the corner of Medina and Bridge Roads, almost opposite the chain ferry ticket office. On the left, behind the ticket office is the firm of Spencer Rigging, a company specialising in the rigging of yachts. They have re-rigged many large sailing vessels built in the early years of this century.

J.S. White's Thetis Dock, Cowes, 1845 (Allan Insole)

From the chain ferry terminal, return along Medina Road and take the first turning left, Bridge Road. This leads past the entrance to the J.S. White industrial complex. The name is all that remains to record the generations of shipbuilders who worked here. Today the buildings are occupied by a number of small firms struggling to compete in today's tough financial climate.

At the top of Bridge Road, as it bends right, a black hole can be seen directly ahead. This is the southern entrance to the Cowes railway tunnel and was blackened by soot deposited by hundreds of steam engines emerging from the tunnel after climbing up from Cowes Station and slowing to stop at Mill Hill Station adjacent to the tunnel. The last train ran through here in 1966 and only a small section of the platform remains.

At the junction above the tunnel, turn left into Newport Road and continue up hill. The road passes a cemetery, a reservoir and a toll house on the left. At the road junction, there is an entrance to another factory site on your left. An aircraft works was built here during the First World War by J.S. White's and was used to build land bombers and sea

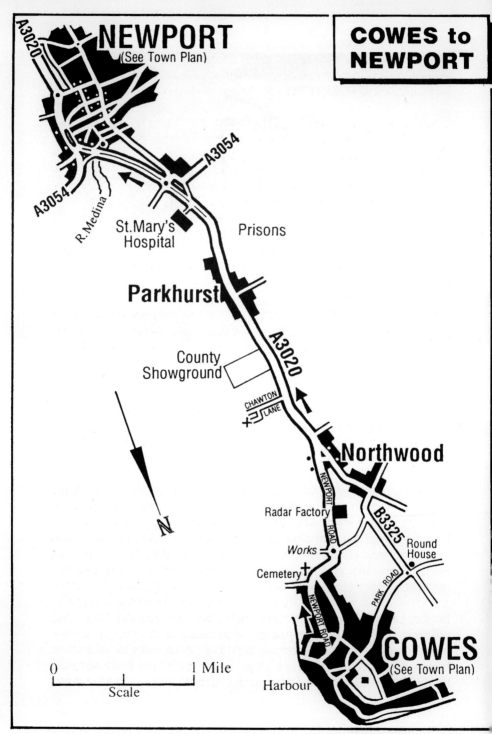

COWES to NEWPORT

NEWPORT
(See Town Plan)

A3020

A3054

A3054

R. Medina

St. Mary's Hospital

Prisons

Parkhurst

A3020

County Showground

CHAWTON LANE

Northwood

NEWPORT ROAD

B3325

Radar Factory

Round House

Works

PARK ROAD

Cemetery

NEWPORT ROAD

COWES
(See Town Plan)

Harbour

N

0   1 Mile
Scale

planes. The former were tested at the Somerton airfield on the opposite side of the road (now occupied by Siemens Plessey). Later the factory was used to manufacture marine engines and then electric cars.

Continue along the Newport Road, past the Siemens Plessey radar factory on the right and through Northwood. About half a mile after the Northwood traffic lights, a turning on the left, Chawton Lane, leads down to the isolated church of St. John the Baptist. Northwood began as a hamlet of small farms won land from the Forest of Parkhurst. The original settlement lay around the old church and it was only later that its centre migrated to the top of the hill. The spire of the church is comparatively new, being built in 1864, but the church is basically Norman. Among the items of interest are the barrel vaults in the churchyard and a recently discovered ancient font. Chawton Farm nearby is mentioned in records of 1248.

From the peace of old Northwood, return to the bustle of the main road into Newport. The road runs down a long gentle incline through ribbon development into Parkhurst. Near the bottom of the hill, there is a broad area of grass on the right-hand side of the road. A lay-by on the left provides a convenient place to park. Looking back up the hill, the row of houses can be seen above the green. These were built to house officers serving at the Albany Barracks. The barracks were built in 1798 and were originally called Parkhurst Barracks, but the name was later changed as a compliment to the Duke of York and Albany, brother of George IV and Commander-in-Chief of the Army.

The first time the Island was used to confine large numbers of prisoners was in 1809 when the hulks *Buffalo* and *Dido* were moored at the mouth of the Medina. By 1838 Albany Barracks had been vacated by the Army. It was decided that the hospital wing should be made into a training prison for boys who would otherwise be kept on the hulks in Portsmouth Harbour until they were old enough to be transported to Australia. The new prison provided an education which included practical farm work, carpentry and brick laying. By 1847 new buildings were constructed for the 620 boys. Between 1842 and 1852 fifteen hundred Parkhurst boys were sent to Australia.The buildings were used in this way until 1864, when Parkhurst briefly became a women's prison. In 1867, Parkhurst began its role as a prison for men. Today, there are three separate prisons here for different categories of prisoners: Albany, Parkhurst and Camp Hill.

From Parkhurst, continue on past the prisons to reach the point where the road becomes a dual carriageway. At this point, on the left is the glittering silver space capsule of the recently built St. Mary's Hospital main building. South of the new hospital buildings and near a large roundabout are a group of older buildings. This complex was The House of Industry. The Isle of Wight was one of the first places in Britain where all the parishes combined together to build a large workhouse for the paupers, people without means of supporting themselves. This was opened in 1774 and could house 600 "Indoor Poor". Many of the inmates worked at weaving and sewing clothes for the workhouse, others at cleaning and cooking. The manufacture of sacks for grain and flour found a ready market in Newport and several inmates were hired out as "home helps". Within the building were sitting rooms for the aged and infirm and schools for the children. The House of Industry was expanded in 1880, but an extensive wing housing spinning and weaving rooms has since been demolished. More recently, the hospital has adapted the remaining structure for its purposes.

From the large roundabout beside the hospital, a half mile stretch of four lane highway leads back to the centre of Newport. So far, this is the only section of such a road on the Island. It is a far cry from the majority of Island roads and lanes, which are sometimes merely cart tracks covered by tarmac and have frequently been eroded below the level of the surrounding land by centuries of use. These lanes are constant reminders of the true nature of Island history as a fertile, thriving and much valued breadbasket inhabited by a mixture of industrious and ingenious people.

BOOKLIST

Between twenty and thirty new books about the Island are published annually. This list is not exhaustive and inevitably contains titles that are currently out of print. A directory of bookshops from which these may be sought is provided below.

Adams, R.B. 1986. *Red Funnel and Before.* Kingfisher Railway Productions.
Allen , P.C. & MacLeod, A.B.1986. *Rails in the Isle of Wight.* (2nd. edn.) David & Charles.
Baldwin, G. & Anker, R. 1977. *Ghosts of the Isle of Wight.* G. Baldwin.
Baldwin, Gay 1993. *More Ghosts of the Isle of Wight.* G. Baldwin.
Baldwin, Gay 1994. *Ghosts 3.* G. Baldwin.
Baldwin, Gay 1994. *Newport Ghost Walk.* G. Baldwin.
Basford, H.V. 1980. *The Vectis Report.* Isle of Wight County Council.
Basford, V. 1989. *Historic Parks and Gardens of the Isle of Wight.* Isle of Wight County Council.
Blackburn, A. & Mackett, J. 1971. *The Railways and Tramways of Ryde.* Town & Country Press Ltd.
Blackburn, A. & Mackett, J. 1988. *Freshwater, Yarmouth and Newport Railway.* (2nd. Edn.) Forge Books.
Blackmore, T. & Orton, I. 1979. *Newport Past and Present.* Isle of Wight County Council.
Boynton, L. 1973. Shanklin: *A pictorial history 1700-1900.* L. Boynton.
Brading, R. 1990. *East Cowes & Whippingham,1303 - 1914.* R. Brading.
Brading, R. 1990. *East Cowes & Whippingham, 1915 - 1939.* R. Brading.
Brading, R. 1994. *(West) Cowes & Northwood,1750 - 1914.* R. Brading.
Bradley, D.L. 1982. *A Locomotive History of Railways on the Isle of Wight.* The Railway Correspondence and Travel Society.
Brinton, M. 1987. *Farmhouses & Cottages of the Isle of Wight.* Isle of Wight County Council.
Brinton, R. 1985. *Ryde Through the Lens of William Hogg.* Isle of Wight County Council.
Brinton, R. 1992. *Edwardian Island: The Isle of Wight Photographs of Frederick Broderick.* Dovecote Press.
Brinton, R. 1994. *Victorian Island: The Isle of Wight in Victorian Photographs.* Dovecote Press.
Britton, A. 1983. *Once Upon a Line: Reminiscences of the Isle of Wight Railways. Volume One.* Oxford Publishing Co.

Britton, A. 1984. *Once Upon a Line: Reminiscences of the Isle of Wight Railways. Volume Two.* Oxford Publishing Co.

Britton, A. 1990. *Once Upon a Line: Reminiscences of the Isle of Wight Railways. Volume Three.* Oxford Publishing Co.

Britton, A. 1994. *Once Upon a Line: Reminiscences of the Isle of Wight Railways. Volume Four.* Oxford Publishing Co.

Cantwell, A. 1985. *Fort Victoria: 1852-1969.* Isle of Wight County Council.

Cantwell, A. 1985. *Freshwater Redoubt.* The Redoubt Consultancy.

Cantwell, A. & Sprack, P. 1986. *The Needles Defences 1525-1956.* The Redoubt Consultancy.

Cantwell, A. & Sprack, P. (n.d.). *Puckpool Battery.* The Redoubt Consultancy.

Caws, S. 1989. *The Isle of Wight: A Pictorial History.* Phillimore.

Caws, S. 1992. *Gurnard: A Village and its Church.* All Saints Parochial Church Council, Gurnard.

Caws, S. & Brinton, R. 1983. *Cowes and East Cowes Past and Present.* Isle of Wight County Council.

Caws, S. & Brinton, R. 1984. *Coastal Wight.* Isle of Wight County Council.

Chambers, V. 1985. *Inns and Ale Bonchurch to Chale.* Ventnor and District Local History Society.

Chambers, V. 1988. *Old Men Remember: Life on Victoria's Smaller Island.* Ventnor and District History Society.

Charles, A. 1986. *The Isle of Wight Coastal Path.* Thornhill Press.

Cheverton, R.J. & Matthews, S.L. 1975. *Memories of Old Seaview.* Richards Printers.

Cotton, G.E. 1974. *Fifty Years of Yarmouth I.W. Lifeboats.* G.E. Cotton.

Cotton, G.E. 1995. *Yarmouth: A Pictorial History.* PM Colour.

Couling, D. 1978. *An Isle of Wight Camera 1856-1914.* Dovecote Press.

Couling, D. 1982. *An Isle of Wight Camera 1914-1945.* Dovecote Press.

Davies, K. 1982. *Solent Passages and their Steamers 1820-1981.* Isle of Wight County Press.

Davies, K. 1992. *Sandown: An Island's Airport.* Niche Publications.

Davies, K. 1992. *Solent Area Ferries and the Vectis Connections.* Niche Publications.

Deare, Ian. 1985. *The Royal Yacht Squadron 1815-1985.* Stanley Paul & Co. Ltd.

Deare, Ian. 1988. *The Great Days of Yachting from the Kirk Collection.* B.T. Batsford Ltd.

Dicks, B. 1979. *The Isle of Wight.* David & Charles.

Dowling, R.F.W. 1978. *Smuggling on Wight Island.* Clarendon Press.

East Cowes Heritage. 1994. *Discovering East Cowes.* Island Books.

Ednay, P. 1994. *H.R.H. Princess Beatrice: Island Governor.* Vectis Research.

Eldridge, R.J. 1952 (reprinted 1982). *Newport Isle of Wight in Bygone Days.* Isle of Wight County Press.

Ellis, M. (Ed.). 1978. *Water and Wind Mills in Hampshire and the Isle of Wight.* Southampton University Industrial Archaeology Group.

Fairclough, T. & Willis, A. 1975. *Southern Steam on the Isle of Wight.* D. Bradford Barton Co.

Frost, R. 1980. *Isle of Wight Mysteries.* W.J. Nigh.

Fullert, H.T. 1992. Three Freshwater Friends: *Tennyson, Watts and Mrs. Cameron.* Hunnyhill Publications.

Goodall, M.H. 1973. *The Wight Aircraft.* Gentry Books.

Green, M. 1969. *Churches of the Isle of Wight.* Winton Publications Ltd.

Harding, P.A. 1988. *The Bembridge Branch Line.* P.A. Harding.

Hay, P. 1988. *Steaming through the Isle of Wight.* Middleton Press.

Herbert-Gustar, L.K. & Nott, P.A. 1980. *John Milne: Father of Modern Seismology.* Paul Norbury Publications Ltd.

Hilliker, I.J. 1990. *A Solent Flight.* Kingfisher Publications.

Hinton, B. 1990. *Nights in White Satin - An Illustrated History of the Isle of Wight Pop Festivals.* Isle of Wight County Council.

Hinton, B. 1992. *Immortal Faces: Julia Margaret Cameron on the Isle of Wight.* Isle of Wight County Press/Isle of Wight County Council.

Hinton, B. & Manby, B. 1994. *Wight: An Island from the Air.* Island Books.

Hinton, B. & Manby, B. 1995. *Wight: An Island from the Air - The Second Flight* Island Books.

Hinton, D.A. & Insole, A.N. 1988. *Ordnance Survey Historical Guides: Hampshire and the Isle of Wight.* George Philip/Ordnance Survey.

Hockey, S.F. 1970. *Quarr Abbey and its Lands 1132-1651.* Leicester University Press.

Hockey, S.F. 1982. *Insula Vecta.* Phillimore.

Hollis, F. (n.d.) *To Heaven in a Glass Wheelbarrow.* F. Hollis.

Hook, G.E. 1975. *Isle of Wight Past & Present: A pictorial record of the Isle of Wight.* Oxford Illustrated Press.

Hutchings, R.J. 1975. *Island Longshoremen.* G.G. Saunders and Co. Ltd.

Hutchings, R.J. 1979. *Isle of Wight Literary Haunts.* Isle of Wight County Press.

Hutchings, R.J. 1990. *Smugglers of the Isle of Wight.* Isle of Wight County Press.

Hutchings, R.J. & Hinton, B. 1986. *The Farringford Journal of Emily Tennyson 1853-1864.* Isle of Wight County Press.

Hyland, P. 1984. *Wight: Biography of an Island.* Victor Gollancz.

Insole, A. & Parker, A. (eds.). 1979. *Industrial Archaeology in the Isle of Wight.* Isle of Wight County Council.

Island Books. 1994. *Isle of Wight in Old Photographs.* Island Books.

Isle of Wight Federation of Women's Institutes. 1974. *Isle of Wight Village Book.* Isle of Wight Federation of Women's Institutes.

Gale, A. 1991.*The Story Beneath the Solent.* The Isle of Wight Trust for Maritime Archaeology.

Jones, J.D. 1965. *The Royal Prisoner: Charles I at Carisbrooke.* Lutterworth.

Jones, J.D. 1988. *Isle of Wight and the Armada.* Isle of Wight County Council.

Jones, J.D. 1989. *Isle of Wight Curiosities.* Dovecote Press.

Jones, J.D. & Jones, J. 1987. *The Isle of Wight: An Illustrated History.* Dovecote Press.

Jones, J. 1976. *Countess Isabella at Carisbrooke 1262-1293.* Vectis Lithographics Ltd

Laidlaw, E.F. 1990. *The Story of the Royal National Hospital, Ventnor.* E. Laidlaw.

Laidlaw, E.F. 1994. *A History of the Isle of Wight Hospitals.* Cross Publishing.

Lane, M. 1994. *Parish Churches of the Isle of Wight.* South Wight Borough Council.

Laurence, A.E. 1988. *In Praise of St. Lawrence: A Song at Twilight.* A.E. Laurence.

Laurence, A.E. & Insole, A.N. n.d. *Prometheus Bound: Karl Marx on the Isle of Wight.* Island Books.

Lavers, J. 1988. *The Dictionary of Isle of Wight Dialect.* Dovecote Press.

Lawn, R.T. 1993. *Old Time Characters of the Isle of Wight.* Navigator Books.

Leal, H.J.T. 1982. *Air War Over The Island.* Isle of Wight County Press.

Lyon, B. 1977. *The Isle of Wight Companion.* Isle of Wight Tourist Board.

McInnes, R. 1974. *Isle of Wight.* Collins.

McInnes, R. 1990. *The Garden Isle: Landscape Paintings of the Isle of Wight 1790-1920.* R. McInnes.

McInnes, R. 1993. *A Picturesque Tour of the Isle of Wight.* R. McInnes.

McInnes, R. & Butler, A. 1986. *Shanklin in Old Picture Postcards.* European Library.

Major, K.J. 1970. *The Mills of the Isle of Wight.* Charles Skilton Ltd.

Medland, J.C. 1986. *Shipwrecks of the Isle of Wight.* West Island Printers Ltd.

Medland, J.C. 1995. *Alum Bay and The Needles.* Coach House Publications Ltd.

Mew, F. 1962. *Back of Wight: Yarns of Wrecks & Smuggling.* Isle of Wight County Press.

Mitchell, V. & Smith, K. 1985. *South Coast Railways - Ryde to Newport.* Middleton Press.

Mitchell, V. & Smith, K.1985. *Branch Lines to Newport.* Middleton Press.

Moore, P. 1988. *The Industrial Heritage of Hampshire and the Isle of Wight.* Phillimore.

Newchurch Women's Institute. 1988. *Newchurch Remembered.* Vectis Lithographics Ltd.

Newman, R. 1989. *Southern Vectis: The First 60 Years.* Ensign Publications.

Nichols, R. 1994. *The Diaries of Robert Hooke: The Leonardo of London 1635-1703.* The Book Guild Ltd.

Niton Women's Institute. 1971. *"Niton Calling".* Niton Women's Institute.

O'Brien, F.T. 1981. *Early Solent Steamers: A History of Local Steam Navigation.* (2nd. edn.) Prown, Son & Ferguson Ltd.

Orton, I. n.d. *The Isle of Wight at War.* Isle of Wight County Council.

Parker, A.G. 1977. *The Story of Victorian Shanklin.* Shanklin Rotary Club.

Parker, A.G. 1986. *Shanklin between the Wars.* A.G. Parker.

Parr, D.A. 1994. *Newport.* Allan Sutton Publishing Co.
Parr, D.A. 1994. *Ryde.* Allan Sutton Publishing Co.
Parr, D.A. 1995. *Cowes and East Cowes.* Allan Sutton Publishing Co.
Parsloe, G. & Parsloe, Z. 1979. *A Present from Seaview.* G. Parsloe.
Paye, P. 1984. *Isle of Wight, Railways Remembered.* Oxford Publishing Co.
Paye, P. & Paye, K. 1979. *Steam on the Isle of Wight (1956-1966).* Oxford Publishing Co.
Pevsner, N. & Lloyd, D. 1967. *The Buildings of England: Hampshire and the Isle of Wight.* Penguin Books.
Phillips, K.S. 1981. *For Rooks and Ravens: The Execution of Michal Morey of Arreton in 1737.* Isle of Wight County Council.
Phillips, K. 1988. *Shipwrecks of the Isle of Wight.* David & Charles.
Powell, M. 1977. *Spithead, The Navy's Anvil.* Redan & Vedette.
Pomeroy, C.A. 1993. *Isle of Wight Railways - A 'Then and Now' Pictorial Survey.* Past & Present Publishing Ltd.
Rayner, C.T. 1978. *All My Yesterdays: Memories of a Shanklin Longshoreman.* Saunders the Printers (I.O.W.) Ltd.
Reed, M.J.E. 1989. *The Island Terriers: The LB & SCR Terrier Class on the Railways of the Isle of Wight.* Kingfisher Railway Productions.
Robbins, M. 1977. *The Isle of Wight Railways.* Oakwood Press.
Scammell, H. 1982. *Rural Wight in Bygone Days.* Isle of Wight County Council.
Scammell, H. 1983. *Rural Wight in Bygone Days. Vol. II.* Isle of Wight County Council.
Scammell, H. & Blackmore, T. 1980. *Past & Present Sandown & Shanklin.* Isle of Wight County Council.
Searle, A. 1981. *Seaview Pier: The Case History.* Isle of Wight County Press.
Searle, A. 1989. *Isle of Wight at War.* Dovecote Press.
Searle, A. 1995. *PLUTO: Pipeline Under the Ocean.* Shanklin Chine.
Sheldrick, B. 1988. *Leisure Guide: Isle of Wight.* Ordnance Survey/AA.
Shepard, B. 1984. *Newport Isle of Wight Remembered.* Isle of Wight Natural History & Archaeological Society.
Sherfield, I. 1994. *East Cowes Castle The Seat of John Nash Esq: A Pictorial History.* Business by Design.
Sheridon, R.K. 1974. *Lords, Captains & Governors of the Isle of Wight.* H.M.S.O.
Sibley, P. 1977. *Discovering the Isle of Wight.* Robert Hale.
Sibley, P. 1983. *Isle of Wight Villages.* Robert Hale.
Smith, O. 1993. *An Illustrated History of the Isle of Wight Railways: Cowes to Newport.* Irwell Press.
Sprake, D. 1993. *Put Out the Flag: The Story of Isle of Wight Carriers 1860-1960.* Cross Publishing.
Tagg, A.E. & Wheeler, R.L. 1989. *From Sea to Air: The Heritage of Sam Saunders.* Crossprint.
Tennant, C. 1992. *East Cowes: A Step Into The Past.* C. Tennant.

Tennyson, C. 1976. *Farringford, Home of Alfred Lord Tennyson.* Tennyson Research Centre, Lincoln.

Tomalin, D. 1975. *Newport Roman Villa.* Isle of Wight County Council.

Tomalin, D. 1987. *Roman Wight: a Guide Catalogue.* Isle of Wight County Council.

Toogood, E. 1984. *The West Wight Remembered.* Eric Toogood Publications.

Toogood, E. 1984. *More Memories of West Wight.* Eric Toogood Publications.

Ward, P. 1990. *Wight Magic: Tales of the Isle of Wight, its Islanders and Overners.* Oleander.

Wells, M. 1985. *Farewell to Steam - Isle of Wight.* Rochester Press Transport Books.

Wheeler, R.L. 1993. *From River to Sea: The Marine Heritage of Sam Saunders.* Cross Publishing.

Whittington, C.J. 1971. *Railways in the Wight.* G.G. Saunders & Co. Ltd.

Williams, D.L. 1993. *Maritime Heritage: White's of Cowes.* Silver Link Publishing Ltd.

Willis, C.J. & Roberts, E.H. 1985. *The Lifeboats of Brighstone Bay.* (2nd. edn.) Isle of Wight County Press.

Winter, C.W.R. 1981. *The Ancient Town of Yarmouth.* Isle of Wight County Press.

Winter, C.W.R. 1984. *The Manor Houses of the Isle of Wight.* Dovecote Press.

Winter, C.W.R. 1990. *The Enchanted Isle: An Island History.* Cross Publishing.

Winter, R. & Winter, P. 1987. *Village Churches of The Isle of Wight.* Forget-Me-Not Books.

Wolfenden, J. 1990. *The Countryside of the Isle of Wight.* Service Tree Press.

Woodward, M. 1991. *Bembridge in Old Picture Postcards.* European Library.

Wright, D.1992. *Michael Hoy: The Man and His Monument.* Fernlea Publications.

York, HRH The Duchess of (with Stoney, B.). 1991. *Victoria & Albert, Life at Osborne.* George Weidenfeld & Nicholson Ltd.

APPENDIX A:
VOLUNTARY ORGANISATIONS PROMOTING THE
HISTORY AND HERITAGE OF THE ISLAND

Organisation	Telephone no.
Bembridge Local History Society	874408
Brading Station Community Centre Association	407693
Brighstone Village Museum Trust	740495
Communications & Electronics Museum Trust	567665
East Cowes Heritage	293010
Friends of St. Thomas'	882459
Geological Society of the Isle of Wight	404344
Hampshire and IW Trust for Maritime Archaeology	721243
Historical Sandown Association	405621
Hooke Society	756614
IW Archaeological Committee	721243
IW Family History Society	520493
IW Gardens Trust	740415
IW Industrial Archaeology Group	853612
IW Natural History & Archaeological Society	740711
IW Picture Postcard Club	873077
IW Society	293010
IW Volunteer Support Services	522890
Julia Margaret Cameron Trust	756814
Max Aitken Museum Trust	295144
National Trust	740956
Oglander Trust	721243
R.N.L.I. Bembridge	872223
Roots, Family & Parish History, Newchurch	403060
St. Helens Heritage Project	872800
Steve Ross Foundation for the Arts	528825
Ventnor & District Local History Society	855407
Yarmouth Society	753910

APPENDIX B:
OTHER SOURCES OF INFORMATION

Source		Telephone no.
English Heritage, Area Manager		200022
IW Council Archaeological Centre		529963
IW Council Cultural & Leisure Services		822000
IW County Records Office		823820
IW Education Centre		811020
IW Tourism		524343
Libraries:	Bembridge	873102
	Brighstone	740150
	Cowes	293341
	East Cowes	293019
	Freshwater	752377
	Newport	527655
	Niton	730863
	Ryde	562170
	Sandown	402748
	Shanklin	863126
	Ventnor	852039
National Trust		526445
Tourist Information Centres:	Cowes	291914
	Newport	525450
	Ryde	562905
	Sandown	403886
	Shanklin	862942
	Ventnor	853625
	Yarmouth	760015
Southern Vectis:	Cowes	292082
	Newport	523831
	Ryde	562264
	Sandown	407918
	Shanklin	862224
	Ventnor	852288

Cowes	Charles Dickens Bookshop, High Street	280582
	The Book Cabin, High Street	295409
East Cowes	Katy's, Lower York Avenue	297562
Brighstone	National Trust Shop, North Street	740689
Freshwater	Golden Hours Bookshop, School Green Road	753434
	Elliots Newsagent	753234
Godshill	The Old Smithy Shop, Public Car Park	840242
Newport	Coleman's Book Centre, High Street	525062
	Mister Micawber, Pyle Street	525320
	Ottakars, High Street	527927
	Smith's, High Street	520048
	Shide Books, Upper St. James' Street	528269
Ryde	Coleman's Book Centre, High Street	565222
	John Collins, Cross Street	562585
	Heritage Books, Cross Street	562933
	Phoenix Bookshop, Cross Street	562790
	The Ryde Bookshop, High Street	565227
	Vision Books, Royal Victoria Arcade, Union Street	611431
Sandown	Pages, 53 High Street	–
	Sandown News, 12 High Street	402792
Seaview	Bookworm, Pier Road	612195
Shanklin	Beardsalls, Regent Street	862616
	Morgans, Regent Street	862117
St. Helens	Mother Goose Bookshop, Lower Green Road	873897
Totland	The Bookshop, The Broadway	754960
Ventnor	Ventnor Rare Books, Pier Street	853706
Yarmouth	Holdings, Quay Street	760265

If you wish to help **The Isle of Wight Society's Committee for History and Heritage** in its role as a communication and support group for the heritage exhibitions, or assist or promote some aspect of the Island's heritage, please contact us through :-

East Cowes Heritage Centre
8 Clarence Road
East Cowes, PO
Telephone 01983 280310
or
Isle of Wight Volunteer Support Services
Heritage House, Riverway
Newport, PO30 5UX
Telephone 01983 522890